Reviews

The Strangest of Antics is an exciting book of verse not just for the young but for all ages. Simple rhymes lie alongside sophisticated moral issues.

This is a book for all of us in which Leone Purdy has stirred up a wondrous mix of fun and wisdom. Ranging from childhood humour to adult gravity she shows an amazing facility for rhyme, never at a loss through 45 odd poems.

In 'Mr Grimple and Snooty' with its 33 rhyming stanzas she displays a fine ear over four pages as she deals with serious matter. But beyond this throughout her poetry she revels in the oft forgot of the natural world, spiders, stick insects,birds, even a croc! before beckoning us into her own special self-deprecating humour as in 'Ungainly Pimple'

'why can't you be like my dimple?'-and the hilarious 'Teapot and Teabag', 'we are a great team , teabag and me'; both much enjoyed in being read aloud in our poetry group.

Furthermore its her choice of language, especially her wide-ranging vocabulary she proves herself a word-smith of no mean order.

In the give-and-take of 'Pride' we have the first speaker

 'Do good thoughts ever dwell?...,you pretend you are faultless'
to which the second speaker retorts

 'Eyes, lips, mouth concurring...

 Tacky, brash, hard know-all...

 Claimed them all...

> 'First rate and now a champion'
> Answered by
> > 'Your ego you need to retrain'
> Summed up in her splendid
> > 'If only is not in my vocabulary'

— Michael Fox, an U3A Bairnsdale writer

I was glad that the author had a wide variety of style in which she wrote. There were poems that were short and sweet, while others packed a lot more meaning, some rhymed while others didn't and this was a great way to keep the reader engrossed. I should say that Leone had great use of descriptive words.

"I mused, 'Is this judgement day?'"

—Reviewed by Jess K — Blue Fairy Tales

The Strangest Of Antics is entertaining, funny, joyous, and sad but most of all — clever, very clever ! Well done Leone, a well combined assortment of poems for lots of situations…

we are all looking forward to that second book ! "

—Alison Lewis, author "Missing"

Poetry to me is like a letter from my soul. It should be opened when alone to be savoured like a tasty piece of chocolate during a moment of peace. Leone has created poetry that is so personal, it is like a diamond to be hidden away to read again and again.

With titles such as A Short Note which is a poem about leaving home; Ungainly Pimple — Yes it is about a dreaded pimple; Teapot and a Teabag and Curds and Whey, Leone Purdy is sure to attract attention as a poet who has the ability to write about literally anything in everyday life you can imagine.

She has a quirky style and has appropriately named her book of poems 'The Strangest Of Antics'. I hope all poetry lovers will get onboard with Leone and have a great time reading her musings.

To me reading poetry is like standing in an art gallery and studying an abstract painting. There are many interpretations that can describe what you see and you can nearly guarantee that the person beside you sees it in an entirely different way. That's what makes poetry so personal.

Abstract, quirky and unexpected, best describes this book of poems-go ahead, spoil yourself.

— John Morrow's Pick of the Week

ABOUT THE AUTHOR

Leone (pronounced as in Sierra Leone) Purdy was born in Warwick, Queensland. At 16 she won a partial scholarship to study journalism, but preferred to live life and look beyond study. Working overseas and travelling around Australia, she has done just that.

At age 59 she retired from work due to the rare medical condition, polymyositis. With lots of spare time, she started writing poetry for children and has found it to be very rewarding. This is her first poetry collection and is looking forward to her next one.

Published in Australia by Sid Harta Publishers Pty Ltd,
ABN: 46 119 415 842
23 Stirling Crescent, Glen Waverley, Victoria 3150 Australia
Telephone: +61 3 9560 9920, Facsimile: +61 3 9545 1742
E-mail: author@sidharta.com.au

First published in Australia 2018
This edition published 2018
Copyright © Leone Purdy 2018
Cover design, typesetting: WorkingType (www.workingtype.com.au)

The right of Leone Purdy to be identified as the Author of the Work has been asserted in accordance with the Copyright, Designs and Patents Act 1988.

All rights reserved. No part of this publication may be reproduced, stored in a retrieval system, or transmitted, in any form or by any means without the prior written permission of the publisher, nor be otherwise circulated in any form of binding or cover other than that in which it is published and without a similar condition being imposed on the subsequent purchaser.

Purdy, Leone
The Strangest of Antics
ISBN: 978-1-925230-45-1
pp172

The Strangest of Antics

Leone Purdy

CONTENTS

A Short Note	1	Square Peg In A Round Hole	80
Words	7	Treehouse	84
Mr Grimple and Snooty	9	In The Cupboard	87
Stubborn	17	I Will Miss You	90
Ungainly Pimple	22	The Snail and Miss Fly	92
Teapot and Teabag	23	Pride	96
Rickety and Rusty	27	Rude Impatient Red	100
Anything	30	Stinging Bee	106
Secrets	33	Expectations	108
Pink Hat	36	Barnyard Haven	113
Evil House	40	I A-pol-o-gise	118
The Laughing Robber	45	Sausage and Bacon	121
Curds and Whey	47	Catch Me If You Can	125
Shoe Falling Off My Foot	49	Fly In My Soup Bowl	130
When Dad Did The Mowing	51	The Irritating Horse	132
Little Brown Eyes	56	Harriet	135
My Clothes	61	Snake and the Cricket Bat	138
Forgetful Dwarf	63	The Bike Ride	143
But I Thought	68	Four Fingered Loui	146
The Bull and the Ant	71	The Meeting	150
Little White Cloud Lost	74	Tweaks	156
The Journey	78		

A Short Note

As I slowly read my short note
Excitement is scarcely remote
Nine years old and I am bold
No more teddy bears, I scold
Chores are done, it's time to go
Inviting shores, hearts aglow

With raging fire inside, I lament
My fears will be my discontent
I love you Mum, I hope you know
But I have to go, deeds to sow
Join the crusades along the way
Become a fighter, never betray

Staring at my leather cherry stones
Terracotta horse and knucklebones
Wooden chess board, cup and ball
Clay marbles, in my mother's shawl
Tears again surged into a downfall
It was like being hit by a cannonball

I leave home in the dead of night
My horse anticipating the fight
Quivering cold sweat, all aglow
Angst mercifully does not show
Constriction in my bloated throat
I heave up my bulky, heavy coat

Galloping into the murky gloom
So drenched to the core I fume
I put my childish toys far away
But cannot keep this fear at bay
They afford me peace of mind
Teeth, from fear, grind and bind

As nightfall came, all went well
Camp was made, I felt like hell
And standing quiet and serene
A beautiful palomino was seen
Clearly appeared content to stay
I mused, 'Is this judgement day?'

A Short Note

Sword shined in the darkness
And I remembered the *Argus*
Left to last was the youngest
The task became humongous
My hand rose up amidst jeers
I surveyed my scornful peers

In silence, I withdrew the sword
With certainty and full accord
They gasped, bowed their heads
The searing blazes of light spread
Across the sky in golden threads
Tiers of light flew over my head

I'm captain of the great sailboat
Time and love my men promote
Steady and silent, as she weaves
In slow repose the ocean heaves
With honour, loyalty, and precision
They are waiting on my decision

Sailing through fair trade winds
Make peace with the Amerinds
March into the forbidden lands
Villains give up unfair demands
We'll fight in spirit and passion
If rough, there'll be compassion

My demons, I've brought to heel
Overcome, they're now like steel
Lords and masters they entreat me
To marry their daughters, please –
'Gold and jewellery beyond dreams!'
Begging, as their wealth gleams

I drink my glass of sweet sapote
And while not being one to gloat
I notice my burned, searing scars
Underneath these heavenly stars
Sun, moon, the universe, this earth
What is our freedom really worth?

A maiden by chance was crying
Alone in the thicket she's lying
With teardrops sweeping down
I lifted her up, spied her gown
Dirty and torn, briar and barbs
She'll now be held with regard

Outrage filled my young bones
Shiny flaxen hair on wet stones
A peaceful life she'll now lead
A wife for me, will it be agreed
No more the pain and bruising
Her life will be of her choosing

I will be a caring, liberal husband
So compassionate and trusted
To retake, make the devil shake
And kill the foul-smelling snake
Evil won't participate
This land becomes our keepsake

Night is upon me, I am carefree
I know I'll fight across the seas
Looking forward to tugs of war
Racing into the growing uproar
Sandwich is made ready to eat
Ham and pickles is really neat

The pen falls quietly to the floor
Light is dim, he's safe once more
Eyes soon close with no protests
With his dreams at rest, I profess
This little boy so mild and small
Walked before he even crawled.

Words

All these funny little trifling letters
I'm advised from my learned betters
Are so important and have feelings
'Fancy,' I say, as I look at the ceiling
I read at school but hear the jeering
Small letters I see but so awfully late
Jumbled and nonsensical – oh mate
A fish I can usually very quickly bait
But to make a word, just any word
My brain takes an age, it's so absurd

Pint-sized, short, long, oh so common
I noticed letters falling, top to bottom
Appearing to dance all over my page
So putting them in order takes an age
Acid-tongued teacher stands to glare
I stammer and stutter amidst the stares
Headmaster walks up, close, slow-like
Twists his large head, causes me fright
Wanted so to see it stuck in mid-flight
Ugly, chewed, mental asylum's delight

'You can't read,' he deafeningly raved
Spittle plonked on shoes in a rampage
'Words are simple, you take from seed
Sound them out, let them just breathe
Lips will move, tongue will just obey
Use your brain a little more every day!'
A sharp pat on the back is quickly given
Sent back to class to dour Miss Scriven
And I heed Headmaster's wise advice
Now my tongue is clamped into a vice

Mr Grimple and Snooty

Part One

People beware: Mr Grimple and Snooty are on the prowl
Gossips whisper, 'You can at times see her angry scowl,'
Up and down the dirty, cobbled streets, they silently roam
Law-abiding and quiet, bodies tired, hair needing a comb

Mr Grimple was as plain as plain could possibly be
How you could not in any weather, without a doubt to see
His rotund and ample stomach, so roly-poly and on display
His nose as long as Pinocchio, and he would oft times say:

'No-one could or would be more faithful than my Snooty
Far and wide we have travelled, bringing home the booty
With golden beaches and sun, it's impossible to be glum
Approaching the seafront while clasping my bottle of rum.'

Listening to the laughter of brawling, drunken locals
Snooty slowly lifted her delicate, chocolate-coloured head
And her stance so proud and straight, so full of grace, said,
'He's my master and a merry dance we both have been led.'

Her piercing blue eyes glittered, in the sweltering hot sun
You'd swear they were diamonds, beckoning you to come
Snooty was five-star quality, first class all over
Brushed and gleaming, she was never a pushover or poser

Mr Grimple put his drink down, turning to face the crowd:
'If I told you all of the rabid, hungry beasts we have slayed
You would all scoff and laugh so vigorously, and out loud
But believe me, brothers, we are both finished being fazed.'

Staring at Snooty's highly prized, perfect tanzanite eyes
She was one cat you could never disguise, didn't like flies
Siamese and proud, with her snub little nose pointed high
All they could do was to turn and stare, secretly fantasise

Barman's tabby, Joanna, quietly meowed hello and bowed
Deference she bestowed, as she was awestruck and wowed
Nowhere in this land would you find a more beautiful cat
Refined and unusual, a feline loved and looked at

'Time to be going,' Mr Grimple said, loud and knowing,
'The wine is soon to stop flowing, and the wind is blowing
The night is short, the streets are dark, we will need to be
On board our boat, where we always feel so snug and free.'

Part Two

Mr Grimple turned around to pick up his darling Snooty
But nowhere was she seen, and nothing could he glean
'Where are you, my refined treasure, elegant and hooty?
Time to leave, my little queen, the drink I need to wean.'

Under chairs, tables and stairs, they looked everywhere
The cubby holes, secret retreats, the usual Snooty lairs,
The kind and the mean, they all helped to share the pain
Trying to find Snooty without favour or gain, it was plain

The innkeeper quietly checked all the tavern's bedrooms
Looked amongst the drawers and the ancient heirlooms
Slender little snub-nose Snooty was nowhere to be seen
Tears flowed from Mr Grimple, held in such high esteem

'W-w-ur-wait a-a m-min-minny,' came stuttered words
From an extremely thin lad, Mr Grimple now overheard
When asked his name he stuttered, 'F-fi-fi-fin-Finny.'
Afflicted since childhood, his stuttering was such a pity

Deciding to write it down, it had made him really frown
Hiding his face, the thief quickly lowered his head down
As he turned, Finny saw a jagged scar, ripped and worn
In a silhouette against the light, his face filled with scorn

Finny stopped his writing to recall his jumbled thoughts
All bumped together, as ideas plunged into quarts
Gradually they separated, and went their distant ways
Conjuring and fathoming, unravelling for savvy displays

Unquestionably, this information went to the right place
While Finny would in urgency and haste, and hopes apace
Stammer and stutter until he was simply blue in the face
He persevered and the words coherently found their pace

He wrote evenly and truthfully of what he saw take place
A reputation for explanation, truth couldn't be so erased
The stuttering Finny persisted, felt the stress and pressure
This experience would be the making of him for the better

Finny saw him come slow and deathly, his scar blood red
Eyes watching, darting everywhere, was he being misled?
With barefaced joy and conceit, this Finny didn't foresee
Little chocolate-coated Snooty was taken in hales of glee

This scar-faced ruffian had enraged and now upstaged
While Snooty fought like a tiger caged, so very outraged
In a bag she was dropped as she whined so disagreeably
Out the door quick as lightning, and the battle was waged

Part Three

Mr Grimple looked around in hopeless misery and despair
In tears, anger and grief, life was captured in a sombre air
He couldn't accept Snooty was gone and his face hardened
The culprit would be found, and there would be no pardon

Without any warning, the inn exploded into fevered action
A split second, less than a fraction, now noticeable traction
This motley bunch headed for the door in an almighty roar
Mr Grimple and company had just declared outright war

They trampled through the barbed and spiked wasteland
Up the mighty hills and swollen swamps, their heartland
Shouting, hoping, calling loudly for their beautiful Snooty
There was a loud yell: 'He's found, just look at the cruelty.'

Bending down to inspect the stiff, dark and cold outline
They prodded and shoved, this small body full of grime
'It's not Snooty,' was the hardened yell, shouted loudly
Everyone came together and declared relief so proudly

In town they enquired of the violent, disreputable thief
His home discovered, they were betwixt with disbelief
This neat little house in the square took pride of place
Smoke from the chimney, curtains of white pretty lace

He couldn't live here, was the general tone of thought
He's far too rough, possessions there would be nought
Doubting and distrustful, their curiosity won the day
Pounding on the wooden door as if heading for the fray

Warm and inviting, bedazzling floors with brilliant lights
As wife stood beside her husband with no fear or fright
With soft shades of grey and white, her hair sat so neat
While she held her husband's hands and smiled so sweet

'We knew you'd look for my husband to take Snooty back
To have him again amongst the fold, free from any attack
To share with him your adventures on the roaring oceans
To share the excitement and the belligerent commotions

'You see, we found Snooty in the alleyway all bundled up
In a dirty filthy bin, alone and crying, bound up in a truss
He was meant for us and we took him to our lovely home
Healed his weeping sores and wounds, nix again to roam

'We awoke one day to find our house, all ablaze with fire
My husband held Snooty for the last time, it was so dire
In a sea of flames a beam fell on his face, Snooty ran off
Our life in ruins, it was simply too hard to make sense of

'Two years on, a new home we have built all over again
Without our darling Snooty, the intense pain it did send
Look really close now, concerned gentlemen, after all
A more loved or contented cat could any of you recall?'

A generous yawn and her leg she bulldozed into mid-air
A short furry tongue stroked down her soft brown hair
Over her back and her head in a steady swaying motion
The log fire lit up her sooty face, filling you with emotion

Mr Grimple walked unsteadily to this feline of nine lives
He heaved a sigh of relief at this magical sight and cried
As Snooty slowly walked towards him so self-assuredly
Head butts and cusses and kisses, in control undisputedly

In command again and artfully jumping onto Scarface
A deal was done, Snooty now lives it up at both places
With two homes now and a ship in tow, Snooty knows
Which way to go, who knows, no-one will ever oppose

Mr Grimple invites Scarface to sail the seas with him
As Snooty shares their cabins, the lights are dimmed
With mystique and charm these strange lands beguile
Watching Snooty lead the way made everyone smile

Stubborn

Stubborn walked up the mountainous hill
With shifting sands, the steep land so still

Bypassing the hummock, the rising dune
Is it too early to see the friendly baboon?

With a surge of boldness, determination
Stubborn felt anticipation, sheer elation

Told of the booming giant that lived there
Stubborn simply shrugged and didn't care

In the darkness, with sunlight at half-mast
Reliable, steadfast, he noticed the contrast

Long, doleful cries and shrieking screams
How can he sleep, and realise his dreams?

With cringing shadows in the blackness
An atlas would not have shown the axis

Chinks of light sparkling in the distance
No resistance and absolute persistence

Stubborn breathed and wheezed so fast
Burrowing deep below the ground so vast

Now Giant stood still at the top of the hill
He didn't come with any flounces or frills

He refused to move and looked around
His massive feet clenched to the ground

Silence gridlocked the choked, silent air
As Giant stood there, simply didn't care

A loathsome smell, so mouldy and stale
Teeth rotten to the core, as Worm paled

Threadbare and shabby, Giant so remote
His lips moved but where was his throat?

Huge and hulky, he calmly looked down
Stubborn haltingly turned, spun around

Adoring and polished, Stubborn bowed
'Your humble servant Sir, if I'm allowed.

Stubborn

'Please Sir, Mr Giant, I'd prefer to pass;
No need for an irksome, fearful impasse.'

Huge and unshapely, surly and so silent
But Worm somehow felt Giant was reliant

Soaked in mud amidst thorns and leaves
He looked down at Worm and perceived

Worm could have crawled underground
Hidden in the darkness without a sound

With eyes deeply etched into Giant's face
The thick, wart-sodden skin was the base

Misshapen craterous nose, sordidly bent
Face sagging, chin in discord and dissent

Ravaged by time with indifference, neglect
Without compassion, not given any respect

So Stubborn glanced at the giant so free
He mused, 'Would he mind a little of me?'

With courage he asked if he could pass
Giant looked Worm up and down at last

Looked for reasons to say no, and so go
Saw Worm's steely resolve: said, 'Hello!'

Giant knew he had finally met his match
Even though Worm was now on his patch

A curious sensation came over Giant
More compliant, less defiant, an alliance

With folds all a-dither, Giant now smiled
For this was so rare, and Worm saw style

Smelling so foul from top to reeking toe
Worm paid no attention, he just let it go

To know Giant you had to go deep within
As years ago he was banished by his kin

A tyrant now, it became his second skin
Tiny Worm paused and edged up his chin

Everyone could see from many miles away
From peaks of the mountains, to alleyways

The giant's dark shadow towered above
He could have caught the encircling dove

One unusual individual, both so original
Biddable, but unpredictable, not typical

Roars of encouragement not gone astray
Giant moved, to everyone's utter dismay

With storms of tears, now overflowing
Into bubbling, hefty clefts, oceangoing

Stubborn shyly bowed, went on his way
Giant now a friend, forever will he stay

Ungainly Pimple

Ungainly pimple sitting on my nose
So you hope to gain, I will suppose
Upon my word, ungainly pimple
Why can't you be like my dimple?
So very pretty and glaringly cute
Stands out sweet as candied fruit
I am in despair and growing thin
Friends grin when I meet their kin
To see me oozing oily black skin
Bad hygiene and dirt, I do deplore
Always washing, how much more?

Wormlike and black, sitting proud
Destroying my life, is this allowed?
Not old enough to shave you away
My laughter is, for now, held at bay
And with potions and lotions galore
Creams and drops filling the drawer
Just maybe I could go out the door
Hold on there, I forgot the green gel
It will either help or keep me in hell
And you don't give a hoot, I can tell
Ungainly pimple living in my oil well

Teapot and Teabag

Loosen up, it's coming through
Hot and steaming in full view

Don't allow it to overflow
Make mistakes and I will know

Consistency is what we need
The right ingredients we heed

Not too dark and not too light
We need the tea to be just right

So teabag, where are you from?
You're mixed with such aplomb

Aroma is foremost so essential
Taste is absolutely presidential

Every drop is a surety of purity
You possess such total maturity

I watch the bustling steam whirl
Ample swirling, you are sterling

Sugar and cream I have gleamed
Duty I will do and reign supreme

Teapot is my only claim to fame
From Chinese porcelain I came

Simple, so cute in blue and white
Aglow, with such flow and height

Used every day, I will have a say
As free and gay as in my heyday

I'm very much in great demand
My life certainly has been grand

Thus, plainly hopeless as it were
I'm complete, but just need a stir

How I've roamed from my home
Never once used with Styrofoam

My delicate handles fill with pride
Perfectly bestowed on every side

Expertly aligned, so well designed
Poised, my culture is well defined

Life is constant, use is guaranteed
Teabag, you need me, you concede

And as the children poke and prod
Who are they to decide if I am odd?

With sticky fingers the cups pile up
Forever picked up, need a clean-up

Faded and jaded, I still performed
How I wished they were airborne

As school beckons them once more
Edgy and curt, they're out the door

We are both now left alone and free
To view the world, bask on the quay

Eyes light up, prepare for a close-up
Visitors are here and it's a heads-up

All the accompaniments you desire
Brew that becomes like burning fire

We are a great team, teabag and me
To make everyone happy, this we see

Rickety and Rusty

I slowly moved my foot and promptly noted
My eager grandson had clearly felt promoted
With dog-like devotion and sharp detection
He rushed towards me and made an inspection

I quickly sensed impending loss of liberty
In the hands of little dynamo, it'd be captivity
Stiff joints on notice, don't creak or give way
I'm numb and hurt every day, so do as I say

Phew! I nudge away from my electronic chair
Relax in warm spring sun, as it strokes my hair
Little dynamo bolted to play his childish games
Realises I'm okay, to be once more in the reins

My friends have arrived and we laugh nonstop
We let slip the memories akin to a spinning top
With beer and rollies we trudged to the swamp
Lazing idly and chatting, not needing a prompt

Our woes slithered snake-like, squeezing us dry
As we remembered Miss Weed and gave a sigh
This jockey she married and what a strange tale
He won the race on the wrong horse and failed

How about Tippy Sparklee in the light of day
Burnt his hair in science class, no more ballet
We chuckled with undeniable mirth and joy
Finished the beer and rollies, it filled the void

My delinquent heart stampedes and stumbles
Will it stop as before or decide to be humble?
It's best left alone, I decided, to sort itself out
And it'll let me know whether to mess about

My son bought me a lovely, long velvet coat
Keeps me warm in winter, I felt I had to gloat
My hands shake, strength is fading in my legs
Eyes not good, but able to cook ham and eggs

Trudging home on the winding, slippery track
We all sing very loud and we don't look back
Stars are sparkling in the dappling, dusky sky
The wind is high, our faces are hard and dry

Long furrowed wrinkles line the crisp pillow
Sagging skin becomes so thick when I bellow
With thin and wizened, parched cheekbones
All of these limbs make me shudder and groan

My eyes secretively close in the quiet solitude
As twilight coaxes the memories never viewed
Salty sea breezes beckon the bright rays of sun
Warmth and the magic of love is so much fun

Anything

Oh, if I could have anything
What such joy if I could sing
To paint like great Da Vinci
Write beautiful literature
It would have my signature

What a ball I could swing
The whole world on a plate
Oh, if I could have anything
There's no point to separate
It's all free, it would be great

Greed moved like lightning
Riches he loved so striking
Beside gluttony he craved
His untold wealth to enslave
Nothing at all will be saved

Gave greed the cold shoulder
It would only make me older
I can have anything for sure
It isn't vital to even the score
Never again another chore

'I am the opportunity
Welcome,' was the reply
With hands open very wide
He asked, would I like to fly?
'I can teach you,' he replied

While looking at opportunity
Flying swiftly appealed to me
But after seriously considering
With the occasional dithering
Being different is crippling

Next came smooth insight
This I decided I will have
For when times are tough
It will help in the rough
You can never have enough

Oh, if I could have anything
Flowers would be my king
And alone with the fairy ring
Would rest a thermal spring
Purity, nobility, it would bring

Untold beauty would be mine
As I keep virtue and enshrine
While on a mystical incline
Or acquire a tiresome whine
While I indulge and outshine

Thinking of my life so bright
In the muted, soundless night
If I could have simply anything
I would love a plush nose ring
In the morning, go snorkelling

Secrets

Psst
This actually is a secret
You should not feed it
No-one needs to know
Unable to bear it though

I deliver my soft hello
Securely, firmly, slow
Longer by the minute
Magnified, heard by
'Is it true?' I'm asked so

Sympathetic nods I get
Such anger from some
I don't fret or be glum
At times I'm in a sweat
Goodness, is it a threat?

I travel free of charge
Land on a dirty barge
Buffed sun, I recharge
Gasps, raised eyebrows
Looks can kill, I arouse

I say this without a care
There are loads of others
Whose hair I nicely tear
I'm a secret, transitory
I won't subdue a story

Set aside, I'm at an end
Finished, won't defend
I'll come back, they say
You tend to stray, allay
Now sealed, till that day

My time can be short
What about an escort?
Don't undervalue me
Unshackled, I'm free
You could have the key

Welcome is not in shade
Once out, I'm a grenade
Successor is left to trade
No-one is left untouched
This is my secret disgust

Don't put me to the test
You could be the next
Secrets will forever hold
More than can be told
No flies on us or mould

Pink Hat

Pirouette so delicately performed
Whirling and twirling, it adorned
With cute little bows on her toes

Rotating whirligigs, pink hat curled
Masterly pivot, by no means unfurled
Rolling and coiled, it kept on a whirl

Crisscrossing wide streets devilishly
Omit unknown retreats selectively
This is completed with such levity

This demon of righteous respectability
On display, not an ounce of capability
With no agility, gentility or sociability

Wobbling and quivering so violently
It staggered along so very lifelessly
Eyed the whining, snivelling silently

So boisterous, frisky and rollicking
It would give anyone a bollocking
This hat needed a real demolishing

An eye for travel, it slyly peeped out
With dust and dirt there was no doubt
Pink hat certainly didn't require clout

Pink hat at times playful and bubbly
But could be brawling and disorderly
With artistry so near perfect normally

Who owns this magical, eerie pink hat?
Design and brightness precisely true
Scatty as an alley cat passing through

With sharp loud cracks, lightning lusted
Bold and gauzy, pink hat so encrusted
What has it come to, it looks disgusted!

Who owns this magical sheer pink hat
I ask again, would you please answer
Could it have belonged to a rain dancer?

In reply came a deep-throated murmur
The sound couldn't have been firmer
Rustling at back, obviously a squirmer

Smidgens of crusts effortlessly tottering
Ants on a steady climb, avidly posturing
You scoff, but no-one's been bothering

'I can only be me, and waiting moodily
Squandered into ruin, so very smoothly
Used to despair, who will do their duty

'Made from the worthiest of materials
My cloth now decayed and immaterial
Once regal, lordly, stately and imperial

'I'm looking for a kind, worldly master
Who can reverse this tragic disaster
Remake, outshine, take me out to dine

'Is it you Sir, looking at my brushwork?
This leer, sneer and ogle is only a quirk
My beauty has vanished, I need to work.

'I was once a gorgeous deep carmine
Resplendent, superb and so queenly
Now a dirty, greyish pink, unseemly

'Master so true, I was top of the queue
Bathed in scent, laced and very new
Beautifully attired, the public viewed.

'I'm in no mood for gossip or chitchat
I was once used as a simple placemat.'
Who owns this dirty, ill-kept pink hat?

'I do,' came the far-away strained reply
She slowly bowed and danced so high
Sighed, the master she'd happily glorify

Free and beautiful, and so eloquent
Decadent again and in her element
She looked so delicate and elegant

Evil House

I echo throughout the dead of night
With moanings, depraved and hideous
The grimy corridors a toxic waste site
Treacherous, neglectful and oblivious
I am wormlike, cunning and deceptive
In deceit I am astute and perceptive
Definitely not impaired or defective

My rotten doors rattle ever endlessly
Slowly disintegrating and relentlessly
Crumbling, festering, conscientiously
Smell travels carelessly, it is evident
With intent I am evil and pestilent
I am false-hearted and a fly by night
Like a snake in the grass, I stop to strike

In sweltering heat, the ripples collide
As I blaze with frenzied demonic pride
While scorching globes ignite and sear
Blissfully I inject unbridled, wild fear
Creeping higher, my monstrous flames
Etched against illuminated silhouette
Mayhem and pain lies in my cruel veins

My bedrooms smell so abominably
I fully agree and watch provocatively
They are without a doubt the worst
As someone did quite frankly assert,
'Disinfectant is the go,' voices conferred
This house is simply crazy, too absurd
Is it cursed?' they asked, still undeterred

I observed my dirty, broken windows
Would never think to intrude or plead
Large shards of glass simply impede
You pass me by with raised eyebrows
My jagged edges become so aroused
A statuesque, beautiful home long ago
Endless areas for me to put on show

Whoosh, inside the darkened rooms
My battered floors burble and spume
I pulsate with glee amongst the doom
I lazily dance while I croon and swoon
Lechery and dissipation reign supreme
I am lord and master of stinking ruins
With evil intent, trouble I am brewing

Intruders vexed when opening the door
It's now becoming very underscored
Old, dilapidated and exceedingly stiff
It eventually opens, creates a torn rift
I wrap myself around their thin ankles
As my cold biting wind begins to rankle
I cover them in snow and ice so ample

On high alert I obliged and appreciated
To interfere, collate, relate as if fated
Their SmartKnives, rulers and pens
Measure, ascertain, see what mends
I happily followed in solemn silence
I knew my heart, they could not melt
Their faces in terror, my touch was felt

Jitterbugged his hair at his nostrils' pore
Hands numb to the core, and he swore
He screamed, believed he was done for
His voice I froze, solid as a lump of ice
I have shown him he will pay the price
Spooked limbs, unable to move an inch
As hot anger rose within him, in a pinch

Opening up the wormhole, I beckoned
He quickly sidestepped, I didn't reckon
A sense of survival, from deep within
My termite-infested walls, he's pinned
As my slime drifted into the night
Mangroves spooring, seized in mid-flight
Next time they will be unable to fight

A malcontent and disturbed I might be
For a long time, I have been quite free
Moonlight glistened, I steeled my grip
'There'll be no peace tonight,' I quipped
Rumbling, tumbling, I laughed, skipped
Convulsing and splintered, not for repair
In the dark, I am your worst nightmare

'Look here,' voiced so sharp and clear
As I, the dressing knob, turned nearer,
'It's made of steel, you can feel dear
Can this be so? I really don't think so
Darling, it needs a human hand in tow!'
I moved again, so tired of their sputter
They gasped, exhaled, began to stutter

Not one word could they starkly utter
Down the stairs they ran, in a splutter
Tripped and plummeted to the bottom
Just holding on to the nearby column
Disintegrated, ruptured beyond repair
I relished, with riveting intent, despair
Ignorant you are, how easy you scare

Free of them at last, this house so vast
This house I've haunted since the past
I'd been only a little boy when I died
Nine years old, with insolence and pride
Is that little boy somewhere still in me?
I hadn't wanted to die, so terribly early
This is my home, and forever will I roam

The Laughing Robber

Gnarled and singed, the tortured and twisted sky
Angled and hunched, as clouds writhed slowly by
Warped and wilted, the night light lingered small
In the cold distance, this laughing robber hauled

With his crooked grin and dirty, mothball clothes
This young man was soon taken in by the droves
Good looking and slim, he was admirably polite
Looked inside their purses, his future was bright

He lived in their brocaded, well-to-do homes
Dreamed he was like the great Sherlock Holmes
So intelligent, but on the wrong side of the street
His life was not complete, if a victim he didn't cheat

He smiled and nodded, agreed for all his worth
Complimented the ladies, said, 'I love this earth!'
Washed his blonde and curly locks, face shone
In new clothes, he laughed and hence thereupon

Laughing robber ventured into the winding hills
He pillaged and ransacked, loved his wild thrills
Excitement crammed into every bouncing fibre
'Could a life be any finer?' thought the blighter

Pounding along the rough sea rocks, he quivered
When he spied an enormous, giant green lizard
Went face-up and looked down, his first mistake
Lizard eyed him firmly: 'Would he taste like flake?'

Dark striped, all aglow, eyes smiled in shadows
Hungry lizard leapt to his feet, horse bellowed
Laughing robber heaved a sigh of utter despair
Lizard commanded his horse to leave him there

'I've watched you thieving from all your friends
You're a dolt and a whiner, all you do is pretend
'You're well fed,' said with a smirk, a wide grin
Lizard crept closer; laughing robber had no kin

It was soon all around the sweeping countryside
'The laughing robber is finished,' they all cried
Signs of a struggle, with pieces of green leather
'It's the green lizard, he only comes in this weather.'

Around the mulberry pole they sang and danced
'Giant green lizard, how we have often glanced
Have you spotted the laughing robber, have you?
You look so big, so big, giant green lizard, you do!'

Curds and Whey

The cagey spider laughed
In the hot sun he basked
Not one to be coy or shy
Never would he ask why
He's openly evil and sly

So hungry and bored
He eyed Miss Muppett
'Let us have some fun!'
Never one to be glum
As he eyed her hoard

Little tuppet on the grass
While emptying her cup
A dark shadow stood up
Deep eyes opened wide
Muppett couldn't hide

Trembling and terrified
As Spider swooped down
Big scary man about town
Large furry legs and claws
Curds and whey, he paused

Spider says, 'I can see.'
Eyes light up so happily
So Miss Muppett bolted
And her tiny legs jolted
She never once halted

The empty breakfast cup
Is left, but not filled up
She will now be careful
'Wicked, fiendish devil
No sinking to your level.'

Tarantula walked away
Cheerful after the affray
'There before she wakes
I'm fast, so no mistakes
I'll eat curds and whey.'

Shoe Falling Off My Foot

Oh shoe, falling off my foot
Why can't you simply stay
I would if you just could
Oh shoe, falling off my foot

So topsy-turvy, if only you were still
Swaying side to side, having your fill

What do you see, my shoe
In the hubbub of ballyhoo
I wonder why I cry thirst
Am I so old and cursed?

All around, amidst the dirt and soot
Fluttering into the air like a shot put

Oh shoe, falling off my foot
Please stay until I am rested
Watching you twisting, I balk
Too quick, you restless hawk

Is the air cold or warm in mid-flight?
You dive so fast, what of your plight?

Oh shoe, falling off my foot
Do you really and truly care?
Just what is afoot, I do dare
To ask so boldly for input

You'll be tied, string with nails please
Dad says you're as cold as the breeze

Oh shoe, falling off my foot
You're such a mighty tease
I would love to be barefoot
But in this wind I'd freeze

I know, shoe, maybe we will shrink you
You will then stay and not be a rescue

Oh shoe, falling off my foot
Mum bought me a new pair
They are dark, you are fair
I feel the devil, but hard put

When Dad Did The Mowing

Part One

It was on this bright and sunny day
The sun was out, everyone was gay
Dad said he should do the mowing
Mom's face lit up and it was glowing

And on this happy, special occasion
There's simply no need for evasion
The mood was social, approachable
We made plans, it was promotable

Dad wore his old, dingy dungarees
Leather boots, goggles, no worries
Close-fitting shirt, so safe but faded
Now he was set, graded and aided

He stood on the front porch ready
Looked around, his eyes were steady
Mum baked, her pies were in the oven
Invited the cousin, made a dozen

Out came the Victa petrol mower
Shiny and clean, better than poker
Had a two-stroke engine, man-made
Four swing back blades, ace of trade

So with its rigid plastic grass catcher
We gave blessing to such a snatcher
It kicked off akin to a speeding bullet
Attention given thus, and so to fullest

Part Two

Off Dad went and all hell broke loose
Chickens squawked, 'What the deuce?'
As he put his shiny headphones on
The mower was started and thereupon

Dad stepped forward, not watching
Almost fell, white curl grub frothing
Plump, six legs with an orange head
He yelled, 'The grub killer in the shed!'

Cussing and cursing, I wasn't spared
'Hurry or your backside will be aired!'
This possibility filled me with dread
'Grub killer found,' I boomed ahead

Turf was sprinkled, mowing started
And for a time the weeds departed
Then all of a sudden, huge giant eyes
Glared at Dad as the mower capsized

'A flaming monster spider,' he yelled
As Dad's anguish and anger I beheld
A true son I now became and quietly
Picked up the mower so ever silently

He gave me a look, the secret I took
Forever more it was a closed book
Beetles, centipedes, praying mantis
Bees, moths, worms, out of practice

Part Three

Halfway through, Precious the goat
Tried to jump over tables and gloat
A cropper she came, so humiliating
Clint our pig barks, it's so disabling

Ronnie, our darling rabbit we love
Escaped and was found in the foxglove
This took time so Mum went to look
Thanks Ronnie, for the burned chook

With the mowing nearly completed
Neighbours came, problems deleted
Animals all quiet, they'd had a say
They cackled, 'We had a field day!'

Drinks and food on the sunny porch
Family and friends, birthday launch
A barbecue and everyone knowing
This is when Dad does the mowing

With arms around me Dad said, 'James
I always knew my only son had brains
Now you're going off to university
I will have to mow more assertively.'

Friends and neighbours, they left late
A perfect day, no food left on a plate
It was agreed they'll again be showing
The day when Dad does the mowing

Little Brown Eyes

Harry swooped down onto Marmalade
A sweeping motion, rolled and swayed
Nosedived with an exaggerated pounce
Plummeting with grace, then flounced
In swaggered, inclining development
An ornamental, jazzed embellishment
Causing a commotion so very eloquent

Not one to mind his wise mum's advice:
'You Harry, will instead wind up in a vice
Have a look where you're going, Harry
To have an escape plan and not tarry
Dead of night and with all your insight
Without a word, be careful and bright
Give no-one a bite or downright slight.'

Nothing could deter little brown eyes
Cute as apple pie but ears full of flies
He peeped out from the kitchen door
Ears nearly bitten off by Marmalade
Anyone else, they wouldn't ignore
Boss and master, control he displayed
But Harry was cheeky and so conveyed

Undaunted, bold, cocksure and nosey
He wanted to make it restful and cosy
Marmalade demanded Harry 'bug out'
Little brown eyes decided to hideout
As Marmalade suddenly sprawled
His beloved owner would be appalled
Was he really so mean, so unequalled?

His huge tail repeatedly tossed about
Harry pronged his little pointed snout
Common house mouse loved to pout
Snout pointing up, eyes so arrogant
Mind brilliant with no embarrassment
Lunging for his tail, not quick enough
Marmalade secure, expertly rebuffed

Propelling each other and sliding down
To the darkened steps below the town
His feet throbbed, pride never wavered
Little brown eyes toiled and laboured
Small in stature and of modest height
Unpretentious, mature, petite, so slight
Canny little mouse aware of his plight

Tossing and heaving, Harry flipped over
They lay exhausted, still not in clover
With ponderous and elephantine zeal
Frazzled and limp, refused to appeal
Harry darted upstairs to end his reign
Boss Marmalade like a speeding train
With both of them unable to abstain

Bruises, lumps and bumps from both
Boss rejects, hates it, but is loathed
Uneven scraps of ragged, brown fur
Eyeing Harry, wanting him to confer
'A disgrace, a mouse sharing my place
So now I'll never be able to save face!'
It's so close, could they ever embrace?

Sincere beliefs both aided, and upheld
Boss whined, he was so overwhelmed
'We need good cheer, mouse my dear
Peace will be when it's happily clear.'
Without any gall, he tried to forestall
'I'm tired of brawls,' he lazily drawled
'Want to play catch and fetch my ball?'

Unsure whether to guffaw or implore
Harry felt he was on a sliding seesaw
Not knowing what to do, nary a clue
Asked Boss, why did he always feud?
Boss quickly blustered and flustered
Became silent then slowly withdrew
He said Harry should be in the zoo

The truth prickled and hurtfully stung
A matter of fact, a slip of the tongue
'How can I be so stupid, as I speak
Without a doubt it looks pretty bleak
He thinks I have effrontery, the cheek
Instead of a shriek I will instead peek.'
Marmalade inspected, felt all up creek

Mouse, intelligent and slick, sensed
With clarity and fine common sense:
Are they now strained and past tense
With power and pride hand in hand?
'When do we take a longed-for stand
We can share, you needn't jolly swear
House is big enough for both our lairs!'

Mrs Gobblestone and noisy children
Entered the meandering old building
Used to pandemonium and fighting
Continuous commotion, so uninviting
There had been nothing but discord
As they stood in silent awe at the door
Mum and kids all thoroughly floored

For there they were, the world to see
In the backyard playing, so full of glee
Family all in a stir as eyes enthralled
Throwing, fetching the ball so small
Prancing about when either called
Milk and cheese put beside the wall
Boss and Harry both stood very tall

My Clothes

This dress for me is far too long
This dress would go for a song
As these pants are far too thin
They're now ready for the bin

See the stain on the torn elbow
Looks like it's been in the snow
Both dress and pants look old
Do I have to wear them? It's cold!

My boots don't have any heels
My feet I really wouldn't feel
No good for walking in the mud
School would say they're duds

This rough beret isn't big enough
Then again maybe I could bluff
It won't fit over my head or hair
I hate it when everyone stares

My petticoat is ripped and filthy
In the shop was one so very silky
But Mom, I feel so terribly guilty
Dad puts all the money on a filly

Not just any filly for the line-up
She's beautiful and is heads up
If Dad won this race today Mom
We'd be so rich we'd be stunned

Wear your filthy petticoat dear
Too long dress and have no fear
The too thin pants will cover you
Beret and worn boots, you'll do

You're smart, with a cheeky smile
Polite and forgiving, stay awhile
The wood you found in the gutter
Warms our bodies, here's supper

Forgetful Dwarf

Fat and dumpy, so short on the ends
Dwarf stood up but quickly descends

A hard night was had, they all agreed
Piercing and loud, it's still the creed

In full swing, the whole night through
This house of drunken dwarfs so grew

Liquor gushed from the broken crates
As food tumbled out of sodden plates

Hours later, the silent, hidden peace
Smiled to the sun as it shone so obese

Dwarf left his now filthy, greasy lair
Daylight fell onto his sweating hair

He ambled along as he sang a song
Forgetting Dog next door, so strong

Out he ran, slap bang into the dwarf
Followed him to the crowded wharf

Halfway there, Dwarf decides to stop
Dog is annoyed, he's down to a hop

Dwarf suddenly forgets and asks Dog,
'Where are we going? My mind's a fog.'

Feeling all alone, blank, without a clue
He asked again and wished he knew

Dog jumped up and down and rolled
Licked his hot face, he nudged so bold

He barked twice, wagged his long tail
And Dog hoped the answer didn't fail

Boots so full of large and pitted holes
On all night to guard against the cold

His grubby underwear on open display
Dwarf forgot, and people looked away

'Dog, where is my home?' he so cried
Wished his naked body he could hide

Asking everyone where he surely lived
He sobbed, forgot the words, writhed

He looked around frustrated and swore
Turned to Dog again, demanding more

'Can't you help, you ungrateful hound?
If I'm assaulted, then I will be bound!

'You'll be gone, my friend, so very fast,
It would so pay you to be steadfast.

'Here is a policeman, he will help me!'
But Dwarf was cuffed, unable to flee

Hound was taken back to his owner
Greeted with a hug, the trip was over

At the station, Dwarf slowly sat down
Observing the police, he now frowned

'Why am I here, officer?' he asked
As they all looked at him and laughed

A sideshow this dwarf had never been
Now, treated so shabbily, and so mean

In the caged lockup he was so placed
His watch removed, he noisily paced

Unkempt Dwarf forgot where he lived
His mind drew a blank, and peace rived

Next morning the judge sternly looked
At the near naked dwarf, now a crook

The watch had been stolen, it was said
Traced and tagged, the owner was led

Dwarf now shared the overcrowded cell
Unable to remember, refused to dwell

The owner of the watch came to visit
He wanted to hear Dwarf say, 'I did it!'

As the owner threatened bloodshed
'I don't remember,' Dwarf sadly said

Six years later Dwarf was allowed out
He had eaten well and now was stout

Too fat to go through the cell door
Made larger, went through the floor

Five inmates quickly hightailed it out
Confused, Dwarf forgot to check out

A new superintendent was installed
Dwarf forgot, his release was stalled

As his fat cheeks became whiskered
The forgetful dwarf never insisted

But I Thought

Toy car all wrapped for my birthday
All shiny and new under the archway
Next door neighbours had a big blue
Was it better to take or just make do?

But I thought

Home phone rang so loud and sure
'You at home son? Please, I implore
Speak to me Davey, and I promise
Never late again, this is honest!'

But I thought

The old man sat quietly all alone
Seedy nursing home well known
Many family and wealthy to-do
Not one visit or a 'how do you do'

But I thought

My old man looked pretty good
Went to war, did what he could
His muscles still looked sharp
Now his mind misses its mark

But I thought

Piled high with vital groceries
She prayed, held her rosary
The wheelchair ambled slowly
Wallet fell, never found, if only

But I thought

Husband walked in very softly
His wife was engaged, so costly
In her lover's arms lying cloaked
It was not what he had hoped

But I thought

I stood at the corner of the street
And watched a beggar steal to eat
Pie and sauce he lovingly gobbled
Nobody noticed so he stole a waffle

But I thought

We all have these dire moments
When we feel just like a rodent
Tossed in the dirty rubbish bin
Wanting again our life to begin

And so I thought

The cat climbed up the tree
Squirrel chased so carefree
The dog barked at the lizard
It'll rain, as clouds slithered

The Bull and the Ant

There they stood, facing each other
A standoff, as sure as light is day
It is said all animals are brothers
In the warm sun on the steep brae

Perched on the end of Bull's nose
This cheeky ant felt just splendid
Up in the clouds, all day he dozed
The wind whizzed by unattended

Bull's horns were thick and short
Body muscular, a faultless escort
Wanted to be rid of this pesky ant
He galloped, as hot as a gas plant

Unable to shift this lazy layabout
Tickling his black eyes so casually
To go full pelt, make it a knockout
Should it be straight or diagonally?

Not slowing down, Bull steamed
Determined to rid himself of Ant
Into a field of groves, Bull gleamed
As Bull forthwith started to chant

Squalling winds in cold icy rain
Heavy darkened clouds above
Bull spurred on, full of disdain
Excitement kindled, Ant rose up

'Faster Bull, faster, this is the life!'
As Ant gasped for greater speed,
'You're a long time in the afterlife,
This you need to certainly heed!'

All but entering the thick groves
Wind and hail punched in droves
Ignoring Ant with all his might
Bull hurtled forward, in full flight

His unwelcome visitor was ecstatic
Thrilled and jubilant, so dramatic
'What is his secret,' reflected Bull
'Why is his tank always so full?'

'Our lives are so very carefree
I know, Bull, you don't like me
Getting to A and B is a game
You worry, you will be lame!

The Bull and the Ant

'My life is so very short, Bull
While yours is so very long
Enjoyment and laughter in full
Is this way of thinking so wrong?'

Rain stopped, now bright sun
Loitered in the buttermilk sky
Bull echoed what Ant had spun
Looked for the secret, asked why

'Let's make a deal,' said pert Ant
'We'll enjoy the days, care scant
To be my friend and comfort me
Travel this land, enjoy it so free.'

A deal was done to Bull's surprise
They went everywhere together
Flicked the flies, now solid allies
Life an adventure, so much better

Little White Cloud Lost

Little White Cloud, so sweet, was lost
On a dark and hushed, rainy morn
Echoing storm clouds in mourning
They cussed and cursed and tossed

Shocked hail, uttering he won't fail
He'll find Little White Cloud so lost
And will live to tell the whole tale
They all said he's not to be crossed

Jack Frost and Hoarfrost so put forth
Amidst the talk, and now henceforth
Frozen dew drops soft and graceful
Said they would lend a hand so able

So very pretty, Little White Cloud lost
Are you skimming, naught a glance
Amongst the trimmings in a trance
Gliding at such a ghastly, awful cost?

Seagull answered in a swill to gulp
Little White Cloud fell nigh, yonder
Lying somewhere beside the pulp
Leaving everyone to simply ponder

Reginald, the brown spotted eagle
Looked far and wide through crowds
'We're good mates,' he said so proud,
'Something has happened, and evil!'

The animal kingdom came together
Little White Cloud always a treasure
Soaring wide, the small tailed hawk
Was goggle eyed, occasionally stalks

Little White Cloud lost and all alone
Loved talking to the classy firestone
Lily-coated hedges, large oak trees
Usually sat beside the bumblebee

Little White Cloud was their favourite
Never loud, always helped, so calm
Would sit and savour without favour
She charmed and totally disarmed

Her life was active and so very full
She'd carouse with the other clouds
Always gave a saucy, right mouthful
As the smog beclouded the crowds

'In frozen ice,' Jack Frost yelled
Hoarfrost breathed, then expelled
In ice and sleet they had found her
Alive and well, it was such a blur

Perched precariously, alarmingly
On the rugged, cliff-like ground
Cloud lay there so unmistakably
As if fated, earth-like and bound

Swollen, swirling, turbulent waves
Surged into hidden, darkened caves
Panic set in, full of misery and woe
Too weak for the wind to try to tow

Icy crystals so sprite they propelled
Observed Little White Cloud was lost
They sang so sweetly strong to Frost
As raging waters puffed and swelled

Now true heroes, Jack and Hoarfrost
They rescued Little White Cloud lost
Watchful and concerned lying there
Unaware how much everyone cared

Old Man Winter with one large sweep
Quickly swept her up in arms so deep
'She was so cross,' she told Jack Frost,
'To her skies she should have crossed.'

Whizzing aloof like a speeding bullet
Little White Cloud knew she shouldn't
To catch them, the other clouds jibed,
'You will need wings expertly applied!'

Persistent, purposeful and gracious:
'I wanted to be brave and so famous
But the other clouds were too smart
From the heavens I did surely part.'

The sun set with the raw arctic freeze
As it shrieked and clamoured with ease
Sleeping quietly was Little White Cloud
Carefree and happy, next day so loud

The Journey

They lay rested with such delight
Softly kissed one another goodnight
Ready to view the world in a leap
They rushed to get a hurried sleep

Bumblebee closed her storybook
Her face had a distant gentle look
'You two will also have your story
As your father found his own glory.

'He observed the unknown world
As it quietly, gently unfurled
Noted the forests as they cussed
Watched the rain when it crushed.'

Both of them were a joy to behold
Hobo was intrepid and oh so bold
Not cold, but just a tad imperial
Faults, though, were so immaterial

Dashing, although with a temper
Such a handsome lad and clever
Some said he would turn out bad
Father was cranky also, as a lad

Coco was warm, cuddly and soft
Little snuggle bee loving his loft
He was such an absolute delight
Cross him, and you'd feel his bite

Mrs Bumblebee sometimes sighed
Tried not to cry so she would chide
Hobo and Coco took her on a ride
Flew out of control on the riverside

Motherhood brought happiness
An inner glow with sleeplessness
There can be only enhancement
Watching them with enchantment

With her time shortly at an end
Hobo and Coco needed to blend
Meet other groups of bumblebees
Both of them would have families

'Store the nectar for the children
Heed the path, avoid the villain
As time goes, the story will grow
Will deepen the love you bestow.'

Square Peg In A Round Hole

My mind is like a thick sieve
So thick it simply won't give
I'm scared it'll swiftly burst
I am definitely, surely cursed
So I must be the utter worst

In maths I'm a total drop-out
'Geography, without a doubt
Is from outer space,' I shout
And geometry is a hanger-on
It's as useless as a pompom

French is not my cup of tea
Oh, what will become of me?
Incompetent with everything
Maybe I should learn to sing
But all at sea, they all agree

As important as a bay tree
So what about a beach flea
Hopping on an ocean beach
It would scream, 'Breach me!'
I'm more useless, you'd see

Science is now the all-fired key
I always dream I'm so carefree
Miss Shase wails like a banshee
Mouth sharp as a bowie knife
There'd never be a prototype

Hot sun makes it all the harder
With ships alongside the harbor
My dad on his old fishing boat
My brother in the good old tote
Most occasions he's very broke

Clang, schoolbooks in the air
Reality is stark, pretty unfair
Principal sees me, I'm called
Hear him roar, as I'm hauled
Onto the floor, and I sprawl

Up I rise, swagger, try to bluff
Pulled by the scruff, he's rough
Science room on fire, a blunder
'You'll pay,' yelling like thunder
But I was made of sterner stuff

A square peg in a round hole
Unused letterhead on a pole
So cold, icy at the lunch table
Offered Jane a tempting bagel
I smile, but stare at my navel

Old Colin tried not to wheeze
Very slow, unable to breathe
Aches and pains due to fever
Unwell, but a loyal retriever
'Said I'd help, he'd be teacher.'

Now achieving, I'm a beaver
Mowing lawns, load the lever
I nail gun the broken benches
Pruned bushes, mend fences
We work together, in trenches

Carried the timber to the shed
Now measuring the creek bed
Colin applauded, stood in awe
Now I used the heavy backsaw
Sauntering on to the hacksaw

Stunned, this job was simple
Clear as crystal, it was official
My apprenticeship had begun
Colin was happy, a homerun
New science room in the sun

Treehouse

Rugged terrain sweeps across land so free
Wind fevered, at times you wanted to flee
Nest surrounded with corn and grainy brie
High on top of the large mountain ash tree
China is perched on his hairy white chest
Groping wings are narrow and refreshed

His bluish white beak warped and bowed
China the osprey stands out in the crowd
Quickly soaring through the dappled sky
White-throated bird of prey, so very spry
Sentinel of the tumultuous waves
Bypassed the forbidding, flooded caves

He plummets towards the waiting shore
China deftly snatches fish, but wants more
Continuous headlong swoop, he explored
With such strong talons seizing his captive
Heads for home, and prey now impassive
Treehouse of twigs and timber, massive

With dog-eared blocks of wood, so pitiful
He scrunches around, looks formidable
With cloth, rope and plastic, nest is fixable
Caribou antlers with velvet skin and spline
Old wooden stakes but long since aligned
Spume and scum splashed with the spray
And gorse and nettles, little do they weigh

Terrestrial wetlands and off-shore islands
The osprey's lands shone, pure diamonds
Cosmopolitan, universal and worldwide
Vigilant, looks for food, smoothly glides
China's powerful beak hooks their food
He'll conquer to protect his large brood

Utopian, illusory and so very spiritual
His huge nest appears as a round spectacle
Swivelling and swaying from side to side
China cautiously and thoughtfully glides
Delivered his captive to his female mate
Listened to cries he could accommodate

As food arrives in China's leonine talons
Sight is majestic, like a beautiful stallion
Ripped, clawed, wrenched rapidly apart
The hungry family eat with a happy heart
Little babies whistle and chirp away
Eight weeks old and not yet fully astray

Family in their big treehouse, never cold
Away from many predators, riskily bold
Food ample, large rivers to quickly hunt
Wild, stormy oceans out of their control
The pursuit of game a success to behold
They love it here, their safe stronghold

Little treehouse now so wide and very tall
Accommodates the family for one and all
Babies due soon, in the glow of the moon
With a home so secure it is clearly a boon
Walls so thick and compact, reign supreme
Protected and admired, spirited and serene

In The Cupboard

Radiant gold sequins beamed in the night
Tinsel lighting, lit up so exquisitely bright
Frippery galore with gimcracks fully laden
Trimmings and braid like a beautiful maiden

Arabesque, with such embellishing finery
A titillating, 'Wait and see, look inside me
Full and juicy I am, as any stately winery,'
As the voice resonated thin and spidery

Pretty little Anna loved the gilt parquetry
With its extravagance, fine marquetry
Dark shadows meandering down slowly
Uttering, 'Come inside, and we'll be cosy.'

Eerie, shrieking sounds from deep inside
In the cupboard of ill repute, they so bide
Spider web impenetrable, hardened steel
Sticky and thick, prey ready for the meal

Voices within whimpered in torment
Loathsome cupboard screeched to vent
Spider let it be known he was hell-bent
With turbulence and fierceness he spent

While frozen with fear she could hear
Her parents ever so undeniably clear:
'Please get us out of here, please dear,'
As the cupboard broke into wild cheer

Camouflaged by the whimpering cries
Spider let fly, flew high to cut the ties
Lights off, his web spread like death
The room swivelled, gushed and bled

As Anna opened the cupboard door
The darkness revealed nothing more
To gain the upper hand Anna yelled,
'What do you want?' The room swelled.

'What must I do to rid myself of you?
I want my parents without further ado
Will you grant me my wishes so true
Or would you rather end up in a zoo?'

Seething cupboard choked every pore
Smoke belched out from its very core
Spitting out venom, it fell on the floor
Refusing to answer, it clamoured more

The windows curdled and congealed
Floor broke apart, room a minefield
Fear and loathing, the smashed door
Spider lunged at Anna for an encore

Thunderstorm and hail rained down
Shrieking, decayed, faceless clowns
Stopped her every step amidst cheers
Knifed terror punched her vivid fears

Anna grasped the turbulent cupboard
Touched the frenzied, black buzzard
Kissed so lightly the repugnant spider
With spiralling shadows alongside her

Darkness knew, saying quietly 'adieu'
A small voice, 'Anna, can that be you?'
Abracadabra, lights no more askew
Together once more, a family anew

While admiring the golden cupboard
It slowly opened its sparkling door
Revealing a brilliant, radiant diamond
Sitting on its magical, mystical floor

I Will Miss You

Before I go so far away
I wanted to firstly say
Just what's in my heart
Right from the very start

So I thought I'd write
The words in the sky
But what if the wind
Had said 'goodbye'

I'll write it in the sand
But the incoming tide
Won't let them stand
This I took in my stride

To hide a note in your bag
You might think I'm a dag
Maybe a letter in the post
As it travels the Ivory Coast

A text I could send from me
While beside the fig tree
Others might likewise see
Love I promised so carefree

A poem I must clearly write
Words not long, just right
But will it say what I feel
Not cover up or conceal?

As I search your eager face
I realise there is no place
I'll tell you now before I go:
'I love you, will miss you so.'

The Snail and Miss Fly

'Oh give me a ride please, Miss Fly
You're so fast, this you cannot deny
And you fly with the finest of ease
Clumsy, slow, I drag and crawl half-mast
Slide on one foot – I can't swim fast!

'Oh, give me a ride please, Miss Fly
And I would gladly say goodbye
To life here as I run away with you
My plight is true and I really need you
I would wait endlessly in the queue!'

Tiny Fly listened without any blinking
Attentively, quietly, patiently thinking
Her feathery light wings were full size
With large fawn-like eyes, she's so wise
And observed Snail's weeping and tries:

'Oh please, take me to a faraway land
One so different, wouldn't it be grand?
To the wild rivers and rugged gorges
Where I would be at peace to forage
And sing with the cockatoos in chorus!

'Protected from fire, I would never tire
I could inquire about the low quagmire
I'd be careful of the rampant campfires
Visit the hawks, parrots and pretty owls
And never would I even think to scowl.

'Oh please, do give me a ride, Miss Fly
For is it too much to ask, I need an ally
Torrential rains will flood my home
With the burning desert I can't roam
I would be better off as a rhizome!'

Confused, Fly answered weeping Snail,
'The rains will stop, so no need to wail
It'll become dry once more, dear Snail
You have a hardy shell and good jaws
Powerful teeth, so why at all withdraw?

'A diverse land will have many flaws
And I pause because of probable cause
I'm sorry Snail, for no such applause
But I really simply don't understand,'
Fly remarked, as in a stern reprimand

Snail persevered, looked at Miss Fly
'I could protect you from any prey
You might hide underneath me, I say
And no-one would even see you there.'
But Fly just didn't seem to care

With the billowy wind in her face
Fly crisscrossed the sky with grace
Snail still hadn't learnt and Fly sighed
A storm was brewing from up high
Snail saw Fly, drifting like a butterfly

As thunder rolled from miles away
Desperate Snail decided to convey
Nervous and anxious he now waited
To explain his problem as translated,
'I feel, Fly, so frustrated and ill-fated.'

As Fly perceptively listened to Snail
She was conscious of a sad and sorry tale
'My beloved has in truth forsaken me
So to a land where I can disappear
Away from everything I hold so dear.'

With tears in her eyes and sympathetic ear
Fly whisked Snail to an exotic hemisphere
'A special place just for you, dear Snail
You'll find your true love, you won't fail.'

Pride

My name is Pride and with joy
My inner self is usually coy
According to simply everyone
People have much more fun
To take control, I am undone
Want to pinch my ample bum
It is jolly large, I say old chum

It's as deep as a depth charge
Homely barge with surcharge
Someone said out loud 'winch'
I refused to budge or squinch
Can't you change just a little?'
Bum leered, snorted up spittle
My heart ached, I felt brittle

Smaller size was warily advised
Bum would look so very stylised
This made Bum cold and steely
'Does it really matter?' I said freely
'You are who you really are, Bum
In this cold and wintry weather
Think of keeping warm together!'

A sneering voice I could hear
I so wished it would disappear
Surely I needed to rightly flee
But flashy Pride won't let me
'Lying, hiding, watch as you go
You're just another stale Joe,'
Cynical voice said so very low

'Far too hard to sell, or expel
Do good thoughts ever dwell?
Needed is grace and softness
You pretend you are faultless
You are a rare gem, flawless
Arms never holding, so snide
This and more is but a guide.

'Eyes, lips, mouth concurring
Rough stirring, no yearning
Tacky, brash, hard, know-all
Beachball, football, softball
To the harsh, outside world
Claimed them all, selfish churl
Could have been such a pearl.

'First rate and now a champion,'
Uttered with mocking disdain,
'Your ego you need to retrain.'
But Pride refused to take blame:
'Hard work has developed me.'
To a sneering voice, I say surly,
'*If only* is not in my vocabulary!'

'Sneering voice, you're jealous
As a hungry cricket on a trellis
You expect me to simply beg
To be satisfied with the dregs?
Show yourself, sarcastic voice!
I can't see you, only hear you
Somewhere within, as if on cue.'

'You say I am saucy, conceited
Spiteful, arrogant and brassy
You say I cheat, I'm so crafty
I so long for you to go to hell
Mock me relentlessly, I'll tell
When others aspire to be me
They blissfully try devotedly.'

My piercing loud voice booms
Like shattered shards of glass:
'I say, of course I am first class
But my mouth is far too large
One day someone will charge
Nose is somewhat flat, oh well
Can breathe, smell, I'm swell.

'Depart, leave me to my realm
Strong, I'm like a winged elm
I don't despair along the way
Ego is full of self, I'll downplay
Sneering voice, go, back away
I will not take the devil's offer
But be on my conceited way!'

Rude Impatient Red

The sombre dawn approached
Fleeting thick fog encroached
Vaporous, veiled, it was almost
Like the hooded passengers
Bathed in obscurity so valuable
Their desire was undeniable

Commotion is, of course, limited
Turbulence heavily prohibited
With the clatter and the rumpus
There was no time for any ruckus
You are all driving on a new line
And you better be there on time

Deciding to toe the line today
As Red frequently so strayed
Rude, impatient, he'll not delay
Fiery and hot under the collar
Every loud holler, less a dollar
Red the steam engine on offer

Clickety clack, clickety clack
Echoes from the winding track
Horn shrieks, as cows bellowed
Passengers stare out of windows
Engine belches from the weight
Red chugs, as usual dominates

Racing along at an almighty speed
Red observed as if at a stampede
Should he stop for the hell of it
Or miss the scent for a lickety split?
He reasoned there was no need
Didn't he always edge and lead?

Moody and difficult to the core
Short-tempered, petulant, raw
He was always willing to explore
His feelings you could not moor
The fickle hand of luck or fate
Helped to choose a perfect mate

Amidst the clamour, steel on steel
Plumes of smoke flushed the sky
Thoughts of yesterday came nigh
Suddenly Red charged northward
And passengers lurched forward
This drive at times, so awkward

Violet was his, she'd always said
Yet Red saw her helping Stan
Only new and needing to be led
A short time only, you understand
Red would never, no, never beg
Violet thought Red was so grand

Violet knew Stan would manage
With her he had an advantage
Smiling at Stan, not seeing Red
Unable to see him from ahead
Red rumbled into the station
Feeling far from blissful elation

Arriving at the station after dawn
Red chugged and blew his whistle
His feelings obviously well worn
Already wary, he started to bristle
As he noticed his beloved Violet
Rested and perky as a sky pilot

He poured out his heart, felt low:
'Do you love me Violet, or will I go
To a place where no-one knows
Where the rivers don't ever flow
No birds, snow or even rainbows
Barren land only and all its woes?'

He preferred the simple truth
And eyed the smart little train
Spit and polished, his Violet was
A more beautiful steam train
Admiration he couldn't refrain
Violet's trust he wanted to gain

They won't be needed any more
Diesel trains were coming to the fore
Steam had its day in the sun
Time for a different kind of fun
Bureaucracy, when said and done
Never kind, or cared for anyone

Red sidled up to Violet so quietly
With tenterhooks, total anxiety
Didn't look at rooks or brooks
Endless days in the sun he looks
Long jaunts in the countryside
His beautiful Violet by his side

When she steamed full throttle
Red felt nothing but sheer pride
Who wouldn't want a super ride
On a lavender painted steel body?
Bending over, Violet kissed Red
Born and bred to this life she led

Red kissed her back, astonished
Asked Violet to always be honest
He had pride, he quietly chided
If Stan came, please don't entice
He quietly wondered at what price
What would he have to sacrifice?

The fateful day had quickly come
Retired and no more on the run
Red, Violet and Stan do the shows
And everyone forgets their woes
People loved it, keep coming back
Wearing their hats, eating their snacks

Stinging Bee

Nothing that I have felt or seen
Is as painful as a stinging bee
Completely unbothered, free
He couldn't have given a bean

To sneak up all so quietly like
To sting and not cause affright
Stinging bee with all his might
You are so small and very light

Sitting on him and so unaware
How cruel he can be and scare
Intestines left under your skin
Barbed piercing, head in a spin

Attempt to put him in the bin
And remove him, it isn't a sin
He's lying helpless on the floor
Stings you again to the very core

Up I get – in a flash, I inspect
He'll fell your body, no respect
As you head for the outer door
Bee's small frame I coolly abhor

With baskets laden, the children
Wander in the bracken, so tall
Ripe for the spoils, they will fall
You're there, looking so silken

Brightly coloured and oval-shaped
Your antennae is so landscaped
They are foraging on the rocks
Visually discerning, taking stock

No need for undisguised mirth
Warn fully, we'll hear an alert
Guarding your precious home
Now, we will leave you alone

Can we not have some fun, bee
The world is large, do you agree?
Solitary or social you can be
But never will I have you in for tea

Expectations

Shiny the goat was above expectations
Undeniably, one of those rare creations
Made perfectly, and given to flirtations
Shiny trilled, as pure as the driven snow
How did this happen, does anyone know?

His skin a ray of light, filmy and aglow
Eyes sparkling, he will often say hello
With the smallest of bleats and a grunt
Wagged his tail and stood to confront
Now sniffing, as if on a treasure hunt

Never glum, he prefers to be sociable
But facing Spud, Shiny was ropeable
Spud to goat as they eyed each other
Shiny glared, and wanted to smother
Wondered if this spud had a mother

Never before had he shared his bed
His home, farmer Ted or corn bread
He couldn't even prowl on his frontier
Spud was here, and it was made clear
Shiny couldn't keep what he held dear

Shiny knew the time had come to brace
And farmer Ted so wanted this space
It had great soil, was very well watered
The ideal land, Ted not giving a quarter
Shiny, seized by disgrace, it was torture

In horror, imagine sharing with a spud
Shiny wished for a massive, huge flood
Spud sensed Ted had caused bad blood
He wished he could fly away and scud
Shiny was very angry while in the mud

'It has never happened to me before.'
It scared him to the core, as he swore
Men came in and seized him quickly
'This is it,' he said thickly, dejectedly
His life now soured so unexpectedly

A bristly temper you can't cut through
Jumbled thoughts he couldn't subdue
As spuds everywhere grew and grew
Farmer Ted quietly looked at the view
Shiny reflected, 'What else would ensue?'

Expectations of course, are the ignition
And with apprehension, and suspicion
They became an unwanted admission
But Ted was slippery as a politician
Shiny now had a pretty new addition

Annabel stood looking a little unsure
Silently cried, needed to be reassured
Shiny strolled over slowly, a leftover
She wondered if this would be clover
As, surly and scowling, he walks closer

'Hmm,' her figure he noticed, 'great,
And she clearly watches her weight,'
When nervous, Annabel will faint
She needed to inspect and acquaint
Cute little goat, you couldn't berate

Annabel's eyes noted the surly Shiny
He deliberated, ever so icily,
'Maybe it's for the best, I'll be blessed.'
And he decided to put her to the test
To set his troubled, cold mind at rest

Shiny was actually in all of a flutter
And expressed an eager, keen wish:
'We need to get to know each other
So Annabel, first of all, I'd like a kiss.'
She sidled beside Shiny – oh, what bliss!

'To scour the meadows would be fun
A swim in the lake would be a home run
Flush out snails, ants and slippery mice
Frolic with the butterflies for exercise
All this and more, Annabel, to be precise.'

Timidly, she looked Shiny up and down
Looked again, wandered slowly around
From head to tail, sideways, back again
'What on earth are we waiting for then?'
As she playfully ran, away to the bend

Annabel would cheerfully fake a pose
Spill the beans, let slip, jovially disclose
Other male friends who had proposed
Playing it cool, not being anyone's fool
Just maybe, this was going to be so cool

Six months later, with an active family
Wishing for nothing, dancing happily
With great expectations now a surety
Spud chatted merrily, light-heartedly
Through the wire fence, so amicably

He too had many family, he told Shiny
With eyes all aglow, shining brightly
And the three of them chattered all day
'Oh dear, what would master Ted say?'
Annabel, Spud and Shiny tittered, so gay

'Will there be any more?' Ted implored
Annabel just smiled, cocked her head
Mooched alongside Shiny, said instead,
'Oh, what a gorgeous day, isn't it Ted
How about we all go for a walk?' as she led

Barnyard Haven

Charlotte paraded up and down the road
Swanked about, as if to urge and goad
Trying to impress, with curls tossed about
Perfection complete, she wanted to shout

'I'm so different,' she chanted so haughty
With an aristocratic, snobbish air, saucy
'No-one else looks like me, as you can see
I am distinct, there's no inter-link, I am me!'

Beautiful and blond, curls out of control
Tumbling down her back, how they rolled
Her bouffant was regal, luxuriously coiffed
Rare and blond, the French poodle rejoiced

While walking one fine, hot summer's day
Young Charlotte wandered the wrong way
Before she could blink, or I guess even think
Well manicured nails were dipped in zinc

When everyone heard Charlotte's sorry tale
Upon her going into a narrative, so detailed
The vet cautioned, the master softly chided
Her barnyard mates supported, as required

Amidst fresh hay lying in the cluttered barn
Rex plunged, thrust himself on a rope yarn
Twined curls spinning, genuine rarity indeed
Checking out the feed, with such lively greed

Give him guidance, but never would he heed
It was always about 'me', refusing to accede
Long and lean, Rex was affable, and carefree
A good mate, who lived by an effortless creed

Sharp words from him upset the wrenbirds
Kingbirds, hummingbirds, meadowlark birds
'I like them all,' Rex steadfastly maintained
And they never once, though, tried to blame

Lovely long legs, with ears small and crinkly
Unable to bear being tousled, moves nimbly
Looking for liquorice ferns, young Rex yearns
Not knowing just who to spurn, as he churns

Rex had walked the long, hard, distant yards
Has starved, been found, given hope, guards
So when it is time, it will surely come around
He'll fight to keep his own treasured crown

Wallowing in the mud was youngster Willard
This shaggy, rugged porker is so bewildered
Out of the blue, he developed a panic disorder
You can imagine Willard, in charming disorder

Princess, the arrogant, red-gold little hen
Casual, adored by everyone, local comedienne
She looked simply everywhere for Rex the rat
Princess loved to chat, chided him when he spat

Princess loved to sing soprano, stridently loud
Her long suffering mates now quietly avowed
No more would she make them totally cowed
Or she'd quickly end up in a very tight shroud

Through the slick tunnelled, glassed cat door
Flo casually walked, the darling we all adore
Long silky curls cascaded to the wooden floor
This dainty little cat certainly knew the score

'Intruder approaching,' was abruptly shrieked
There's a wily fox, searching for the outreach
In for a penny, out for a pound, he'll be bound
He's not making many sounds, in the surrounds

'What will it be,' raucous Princess screeched
Her metallic voice, full blown with overreach
With uncertainty, they all ranted and blustered
Then decided to just quietly watch and muster

It appeared a scrimmage was in the making
Frank, the gaping cow, waddled over, quaking
'What's going on?' he grunted so noisily
Told to be quiet, he closed his mouth loyally

Molly, a black Labrador, went for the throat
'We definitely won't grieve, so fox take note!'
'I'm hungry,' Fox shouted, he slowly squared
'You all have plenty, pal, that could be shared!'

'End this pointless farce, I'm cold and frozen,'
As Frank, courageously pushed the door open
'Before your razor sharp teeth slash me apart
How about showing some compassion, heart!'

Fearful, Rex sat on the back of loud Princess
And Willard stayed outside, now so incensed
While Charlotte fell in love at first sight
The air could've been cut with an edged knife

Amiable Molly finally relented, without mirth
Uppity Charlotte is now more down to earth
Cheeky Fox was asked to stay, no more a stray
Frank had fun with Fox, and they loved to play

Tense, Willard and Princess met Fox halfway
Right of way given, there won't be any affray
Well fed, part of the family, for open display
Fox found the blue seaway, with no foul play

And thus, the happy family continued to grow
Charlotte had her babies, they were all the go
White and curly, elegant and clever in spades
Fox's eyes recalled the lakes and everglades

I A-pol-o-gise

Part One

'I a-pol-o-gise, a-pol-o-gise, in this your hour of demise
I a-pol-o-gise, a-pol-o-gise, there's no need to disguise
The end is finally here and your silence forever more
My short memory will momentarily store, then deplore.'

A swivel, eyes fluttering and a master of camouflage
'Little Walking Stick Insect, are you a delusion, mirage?
You are as meek and mild as a baby lamb, I swear
Delicate, fragile, disliking glare, so loving the night air.'

Spider decided to make his intent well known
Loved to parley, confab with others of the unknown
'I'm hungry, little Walking Stick Insect, the air is damp
With rain belting down, you are looking like a champ.

'I a-pol-o-gise, a-pol-o-gise, my stomach is churning
I a-pol-o-gise, a-pol-o-gise, lush food I am yearning
With such long limbs and theatrical eloquent wings
I am the spider of the forest and will eat like a king!'

Part Two

And little Walking Stick retreated in a calm moment
'Let the donnybrook fight begin,' said each opponent
Spider eyed insect, curious to what it will surely take
To fill his seething, empty stomach without a mistake

Claw on claw, jaw on jaw, spit and grit will overcome
To the victor will go the spoils, the loser the crumbs
While all around the backwoods, wild winds whistle
And alas, Walking Stick now falls into the sow thistle

Barbed and prickly, the coarse shrubs quickly dig in
So, unable to move, Spider has to take it on the chin
Alert to the sharp bristles, he takes his leave, shrugs
He expects little Walking Stick won't enjoy the bugs

'I a-pol-o-gise, a-pol-o-gise, but it was all for nothing
I a-pol-o-gise, a-pol-o-gise, I'm not one for gushing
My little mate so true, my guilt I'm unable to subdue
And my empty stomach is jolting through and through.'

Part Three

High up in the leafy green trees amidst the screeching
Of birds swarming in clusters away from any reaching
Spider relaxes, his body warm from the searing sun
Barking Owl swoops down; he loves to hunt, have fun

Sleeping on the near branch, Spider didn't stand a chance
Plunging him into his mouth, Barking Owl didn't glance
On the ground the Spiny Anteater ambles slowly along
Watches the insect on the large spiny plant, says 'so long'

In pain, little Walking Stick lounges out on the leaves
A huge push from a nearby stick, she was so relieved
Wondered, where was Spider? Would she see him again?
If he had filled his aching stomach, is it on the mend?

'I a-pol-o-gise, a-pol-o-gise,' echoes through the land
'I a-pol-o-gise, a-pol-o-gise, we're all in such demand
'I'm hungry, I'm hungry,' screamed the wolf to the doe
'I'm hungry, I'm hungry,' replied the doe to the crow

Sausage and Bacon

Sputtering and hissing without a care
Bacon browned, and spat into the air
'I am a-frizzle and soft as a swizzle
Cooked to perfection without a grizzle
I certainly won't wrinkle or shrivel!'

Sausage calmly looked on, whereupon
He flexed his bushy top-knot like a con
Flicked his juicy tail in Bacon's direction
Smug Pancetta felt she was perfection
Now ready for inspection, not rejection

Within the hot, crackling, steel fry pan
Curled up on her blistering seared back
Bacon's sides sported tan, but not black
For man's daily dose of bread and butter
She certainly was no ordinary scrubber

And while Sausage casually looked on
He moved closer without the come-on
Doubted whether Bacon would soften
Snorted, rasped his way slowly closer
Spied poor Bacon on a roller coaster

Battered and wizened while she's tossed
Sausage cuffed her over, she's so cross
But was it over-exposure
Or was it a take-over?
Basking in clover, Sausage saw a poseur

Watching Bacon yield bubbles of fat
As she glistened, gaily fell in a splat
Sausage looked tanned and just sat
Muscles browned and buried within
Positively not meant for chow mein

Finally removed from the frying pan
Crackling and brown, all going to plan
Rested and done and now for closure
This delectable and savoury pancetta
Was going on the waiting bruschetta

As Sausage cooked in the hot fry pan
'It's now his turn,' said greedy old Nan
To come to the table and plate withal
To be enjoyed, savoured, eaten by all
He couldn't recall feeling ever so small

My knife and fork poised and hovering
I am oblivious to their suffering
With squeals and cries they quickly call,
'Is this meant for us, can't we forestall?'
Sweet nothings so silently enthralled

I cold-heartedly looked them all over
They're well cooked, crisp and brown
Instead of being wrapped and bound
'Is this all to our lives?' Pancetta asked
Looking around, silence made no sound

Mouth dribbled, slavered and oozed
My heart became colder, I perused
Tongue was brisk, didn't disapprove
Senses flowed with delicious aromas
For to enjoy, I didn't need a diploma

Salt and pepper so vigorously applied
Tomato sauce generous, fully astride
Body arched with crazed desire, cried
'Should I explore and inquire?' It's dire
But hunger was like a raging ball of fire

Sausage and Bacon now lay as mates
On the plate, waiting for their sad fate
My commiserations were just too late
My stomach said it's time to partake
Their hearts began to rupture, break

As fork entered my squirming mouth
A piercing pain lunged into my chest
Ambulance called, I guessed the rest
'No more,' the doctor decisively said
I looked at my chest and felt distress

On the cold, sauce-laden, greasy plate
Sausage and Bacon are now forgotten
Bleak, lifeless, future at rock bottom
They took a stock take of their fate
Who will come our way and confiscate?

Catch Me If You Can

'What a good morning, Mr Croc!
How do you do, from the crew
So fast, I'm smart, move on cue
But sadly, my jaw I cannot lock
In contrast to you, so very true.'

'You will never catch me, Croc,'
As Minnie cooed and mocked
Eyeing Croc's very low height
And with a smile so very bright
'You won't taste me tonight!'

Still waters, blue as could be
Star lights shimmered brightly
As day slowly turned into night
Croc saw his chance for a fight
Wouldn't be obliging, or polite

This will reinforce and enhance
It will not come by utter chance
This will surely be a slam dance
Croc was nimble-witted, canny
Of foes there had been so many

In Croc's mind, he saw them all
At the water's edge, he stalled
Her friends stood by, appalled
Now ready for the last brawl
Careful, Croc is lazily sprawled

Friends laughed and were unfazed
As basking in the sun's hot rays
Croc's snout skirted ever closer
Round the bend, hastily dived
Not wanting to be so contrived

Waiting patiently, water so still
In winter, the biting chill will kill
Summer, you can't stay tranquil
Edging to have his fill, thankful
Waits, hides behind the jonquil

'Ready to pounce, it'll be a bore
A few inches more and I'll roar
Minnie my sweet will implore
Eaten to the core and done for
That, you can be quietly assured

'You're so divine, slim and firm
Will love to watch you squirm
Such tender, curvaceous thighs
You'll cry in misery, agonise
You'll soon be my grand prize

'Come closer, just another inch
And you'll soon start to flinch
Never to frolic below the trees
Never to feel a slight breeze
My love, you'll not be pleased

'Never to dance in the wetlands
My sweet, you'll not understand
It's all in my secure hands.'
She drew closer in the hot sun
Minnie took the plunge, in fun

Croc decided he'd had enough
Sick of going to ground, to bluff
Time to bring her full-tilt down
As Minnie quickly looked around
She felt safe, didn't hear a sound

While chatting happily to a stoat
Quenched her then-parched throat
Croc spied his longed-for chance
Some say it was like a slow dance
Whoever is first, that's perchance

Mouth unhindered, opened wide
All prepared to clench and slide
A more tasty meal, no denying
To push, shove, clench and pry
'She'll tease no more, I'll clarify.'

Bone on bone amidst the clamour
Groans, loud as a jackhammer
Both vying, Minnie a contender
Croc, vile intruder, and defying
This one he'll have, she's crying

With a vicious and savage kick
His neck wrenched and cricked
Croc's mouth opened very wide
Eyes shocked, gaped at the sky
You had to be slick, very quick

Retiring with his bleeding legs
Her friends unite, he won't beg
Black and blue each limb, you bet
Furious and galled, arrogant Croc
Crept away, fighting has stopped

All trace of her soon disappears
While Minnie scowls with leers
Memory of what could've been
Stays forever in his tortured mind
He'll be more wary of her kind

Fly In My Soup Bowl

I see you, fly, wafting about, whooshing and humming
Your tiny body swishing to the beat of the thrumming
Darting and racing, hurling yourself into the clear air
You're flying with such flair, see them stare and glare

You zoom from pillar to post, like a bullet from a gun
Grey and lithe, your small body, shot into a home run
My soup bowl of noodles and chicken is waiting there
How can I dine, while you're swimming without a care?

With your slight hairy body, red eyes and such hunger
Babies now born, you decide to scavenge and plunder
How does it taste –hot, delicious or terribly distasteful?
If no good, the nearby worm would be more grateful

Upon my word, fly, you have stayed in my soup bowl
Fleas, crickets and moths can take a good long stroll
Silverfish, money spider, earwigs with ant
Stealing my food is obviously a tempting, fanciful rant

Throwing you into the pig pen, I do solemnly declare
I'll fight with all my might, and be truly very aware
Swat, bang, wallop and clout, I'll somehow clobber
Attempting to dodder, you'll end up such a shocker

Fly In My Soup Bowl

The sun is shining, the breeze is soft and very warm
Birds are tweeting, there's no sign of any such storm
The next fly in my soup bowl will see a mortal lesson
They won't be here with my informal casual blessing

Tough flywire nailed to all my windows, door closed
And you anticipate, clearly, you'll win unopposed
Biding my time, and I know you'll soon swiftly come
No need to be glum, my pantry waits for you so plumb

In sorrow, this, your day, has now ever so slowly come
Annoying little fly, not wanting to miss a single crumb
A pesky botheration, provoking and so aggravating
Now seconds away from a slating, I'm for dictating

Short and streamlined as you pierce and messily suck
Headed for my bowl, portraying a small sitting duck
Tomato and corn, shredded cabbage and such chicory
Time is ripe for unbridled, boundless so-called trickery

Crisp and sharp, the night air chills me so terribly cold
Gather your babies, feed them from my warm bowl
You've had a reprieve, my pesky, elfin little fly
But don't, for one second, claim my yummy chicken pie

The Irritating Horse

Horse stood there, allowing all to stare
His victories known in the bustling fair

Glossed and immaculate he really was
'How do you do,' he sassed, just because

'I'm very beautiful,' said with conceit
Brushed and perfumed, was so sweet

'I'm so much faster, more intelligent
Keener, and so unbelievably elegant

'I swim the seas, balance on my back
I don't look back, just have the knack

'Can anyone do this stuff?' he smirked
'Maybe just a little,' someone perked

Watched everyone's humourless faces
So Horse decided to put on his graces

Chose to canter, moved really casually
Surveyed the view, noted the jealousy

Reminded them of all his recent wins
Bullies he'd met with naught but spin

'I'm always highly prized, so valuable.'
Various horses said, 'It was admirable!'

'And now I've been put out to pasture
I'm able to graze, eat my food faster.'

With head tossed back, horse rumbled
Sounds from his throat were jumbled

He'd seen his true love from long ago
They had been parted, many years ago

She sidled up to Horse, saying hello
Stole a kiss, and instantly she was aglow

He nuzzled her nose, in quiet repose
Perhaps she'll have to leave, I suppose

Horse and his mates gave rides all day
Folks big and little, so sombre and gay

His beloved assured him she's staying
'Permanent,' she said, happily playing

'Let's have a race or two,' he proposed
The other bored horses didn't oppose

'I think we will,' was the drawled reply
Horse darted a peak at his love's thigh

'You and me will make a great team.'
And his love already began to dream

Harriet

Harriet the red-back spider so small
Loved to gallivant with lots of gall
Ventured wide, and still so further
Beware, you won't hear a murmur

Which way to go and keep it slow
Pitch black, dark logs are on show
Small eyes lit up ready to explore
She discovered a whole lot more

Muddied and grimy, sodden toilet
Perfect hunting ground with spoils
Harriet thrust out her leg, so spoilt
Tasted something, and she recoiled

Panicking, her two fangs dug deep
Venom quickly injected in a sweep
Her victim now would surely sleep
As Dad jumped off the toilet seat

Yelling, Dad looked everywhere
That red-back spider was nowhere
Did the deed, and wouldn't atone
In her home she wants to be alone

The broom was thrashed violently
Dad swore and cursed frightfully
Exploding blast like a thunderclap
'Boxed you'll be, joyfully wrapped!

'So clever, devious red-back spider
In every fibre, you vicious blighter
In every footstep, these you'll hear
Boxed you'll be, and we'll all cheer

'Rushed to hospital, unable to move
Many needles, they say I'll improve
When I'm home, you won't roam
Boxed you'll be, in your little home

'Gum-footed, tangled web so fine
Sticky catching threads with silk
Thy body I'll spread, oh so divine
Boxed you'll be, no-one will pine

'Regrets happen often, you realise
Forget looking for skinks and flies
Red-back spider on the toilet seat
You're mine alone in quiet defeat.

'Funeral parade on solemn display
Carriage and horses pave the way
Her home on a hot summer's day
Boxed you will be without delay!'

Into the clean toilet she's dropped
Not breathing, her venom stopped
'It was so sweet, I foresaw defeat
Not to cuss again on the toilet seat.'

Snake and the Cricket Bat

It was on this hot and steamy summer's day
As chortling birds cackled, fields in disarray
Waterlogged and rubbery, thick mud jiggled
Moths, weevils and beetles, they all sniggled

The rising sun mercilessly hammered down
As people and stock glanced quickly around
Harsh heat without shade and Snake spying
All alone, wanting some fun in the outlying

Snake saw the rock-laden road firmly ahead
In the heat and the dust, rodents mostly led
But beside an old oak, it stood so solidly
Wooden and old – splintered, and very dirty

Red markings, face cracking, the splice dry
This old cricket bat had seen days to glorify
Why was it standing at Old Bulldog Corner
Worn out and jaded, in a state of disorder?

Slithering and crinkling on the slippery road
Slowed at the crossroad, stared as if to goad
Deciding to cross, Snake rolled and viewed
A ravine up ahead, where he'd rustle for food

Cricket Bat glanced to the side and scowled
Writhed from underneath his heavy-set jowls
Ill-tempered from the soaring heat, so thirsty
'There'll be no courtesy,' he stated quite curtly

Snake glided towards Old Bulldog Corner
Not demanding a showdown with Cricket Bat
He idled along – slow, like chilled mortar
Curled his forked tongue, lifted head and spat

Snake quickly sized up the cranky, prickly bat
Without a word, he figured there'd be no chat
His scaly body vibrated in the heat
Pushing off from a rock like a pro athlete

He landed a distance away from Cricket Bat
Held his ground, crept forward on his scales
With a wide motion, bat swung as if a wildcat
Bat always won, saw Snake run off the rails

Bat clipped the side of Snake's lower right jaw
Snake was bleeding, appealing to bat to listen
The conqueror wasn't interested, and ignored
Snake boosted himself up, stiff skin glistened

'Days of greatness are over, mate,' Snake yells
'You've no usage any more, why do you dwell
Forget the honours, handshakes, praise, applause
Enjoy your retirement, please do not withdraw!'

If Snake thought this was making a difference
He was very wrong, and met total indifference
It caused anger and contempt, unbridled scorn
Tasted ridicule, moved to make Snake airborne

Bat attacked, lunged frontward, swinging fast
Missed Snake by a hair's breath, and sped past
Snake retreated, crept around the wizened tree
Tapped Bat on his shoulder, amongst the debris

Snake thrice wound himself around til spent
Said he had no evil desire, and this he meant:
'All I want is to pass you, you churlish cricket bat
How rugged are you making it, is it tit-for-tat?'

Snake's eager plea hit Cricket Bat with impact
His expression spoke volumes, he slowly relaxed
Cricket Bat tilted to a photo at the top of his bat
She was also on another bat, named Aristocrat

Both of them dumped, alone in nowhere land
Oak tree at Old Bulldog Corner, he now stands
For the birds to peck, hungry snakes will crush
To crack and fall to pieces, keep what he must

He'd been rejected, and didn't realise for who
Big wheel in the cricket club and his anger grew
You couldn't be with two cricket bats, only one
The scandal caused an uproar, both were shunned

'Come with me, Cricket Bat, I have something –
It will change your life, you'll be very happy.
Hop on top of me, we will be off so snappy!'
Bumping and bustling, they move so thumping

Sliding over stark ranges and rocky ridges
Scattered trees splash the landscape on plains
Meadows and pastures, rivers within bridges
Roaming furthermost, squirrels playing games

So fast, Snake stopped, and curled his tongue
Smelt the ground, looked for his friend, for bat
Sniffing in each burrow, peered around, sung
Spying squirrel, he talked, bat jumps off his back

Twigs leap from squirrel to Cricket Bat so fast
Big, little, not important, no more the outcast
The dogged heat, relentless and so pigheaded
Forewarned a hot summer, Snake given credit

The Bike Ride

On a warm and sunny summer's day
Where the lilies bloom as they splay
A soft wind blew from the east side
Young Daniel decided on a bike ride

With Mum and Dad both now away
Aging gran continued baking all day
Now deaf, she focused on her roast
Smiled, gave youthful Daniel a toast

Drinking from the glass, he laughed
Cap in the air, freedom at long last
Without a care, he was fully aware
If given a chance, he'd go anywhere

Breakfast late, then feed his mates
The chickens, cows, pigs and snake
They might even want to sleep late
He was fair, and they felt just great

On his way at last, knew he deserved
Brand new bicycle, brakes just superb
His large helmet looked a little absurd
Best to be safe, he carefully observed

Bright sunshine then dull and dreary
Daniel started to become weary
While enjoying his inspiring journey
A cold voice asked, 'Are you worthy?'

He was grimly dark, cold as frozen ice
A fur-coated mouse stood at the splice
Very loud yell, 'Where're you heading?'
'For a ride,' Daniel replied, daring

'You have to pay to pass through here
You don't have a choice,' made clear
The little mouse wiped his icicled lips
Chilled to the bone and his fingertips

Mouse held out his cold gloved hand
And Daniel heard the loud command
Realised his purse was somewhat lost
Questioned how much, as to the cost

Lively and small, mouse became sad
Wicked witch exiled him, he's so bad
Forevermore he'd have to seize a toll
Would Daniel prefer to trade his soul?

Fiercely shook his head, began to fret
Not knowing what to do, he was beset
His money he'd lost, what shall he do?
He didn't want the evil witch to coo!

'Would you like to live in my house?
My animals you can't harm or rouse
Warm and cosy with space and food
You'd never be cold, lonely or feud.'

Mouse said 'yes', waved a goodbye
His life now began to be on a high
Mischievous and cute, sweet as fruit
Mouse now gave the witch the boot

Parents came back, a great time away
Animals fed and chatty, making hay
Chores are done, Daniel earns his fun
Never again would he become glum

Four Fingered Loui

Four fingered Loui was pretty swell
Except when he was prone to dwell
With four fingers on each hand only
It never made him gloomy or lonely

His fingers so terribly thin and bony
His hands, for sure, not at all comely
Mum did clearly watch him closely
But he did what he was told mostly

Sharp and athletic, proud and spirited
Aboriginal to the core, he took the bit
Loui could hunt better than everyone
He stayed longer in blistering hot sun

And holding up his prize for all to see
Four fingered Loui was no wannabe
The matured bream seriously weighty
As he sat there drinking very hot tea

How did he do it, they all speculated
As four fingered Loui was alienated
As the spear was his mode of choice
'It's in the grip,' came his raspy voice

Folks full of spitefulness and jealousy
Made every word an aping of devilry
Four fingered Loui simply didn't care
Aware life was never going to be fair

Multipronged fishing spear and sharp
One end punctured, other end barbed
He brought home a whale-sized perch
The spear hadn't swayed or reversed

This newfound fame was far-ranging
Methods, technique forever changing
And four fingered Loui became a star
From near and far it seemed so bizarre

He decided to go to the nearby school
It showed him he wasn't anyone's fool
Imaginings already widening
Education was inviting, but not idling

Maths he had a talent for, excelled in
Caught unawares, an inclining tailspin
English obviously blessed, given birth
Parentage certainly, no jollity or mirth

Four fingered Loui waited in queues
Trips in aeroplanes had been so few
He said 'thank you' to all cabin crew
Sorely missed his potent home brew

There's a job at the local white school
But his colour wasn't considered cool
Resolve weakened but he was resolute
He's going to work, this was absolute

An accountancy job going in the city
The boss had no wit, he looked dicey
'You've done this before?' he roared
'Nope,' said Loui, and the boss scored

Out the door again, feelings inflamed
Loui felt nothing but sneering disdain
The white man constantly complained
Offering a helping hand was so insane

The community centre also advertised
Highly prized, he was quickly advised
Start-up date was soon to be conveyed
And his talents were officially arrayed

Accountant, inexperienced, will shine
Maths teacher, councillor, in pipeline
The manifesto didn't need technicolour
It clinched Loui as the local councillor

Four fingered Loui was in his element
Silver-tongued, speech quite eloquent
Showed everyone through the centre
Never lost his temper, a true defender

Loui found his cute, longed-for bride
In a monthly local fishing competition
Spear he used with unsurpassed pride
With a beautiful and graceful addition

Nine months later, now newly married
Over the threshold, Kaydee he carried
Kaydee is shown off to all the family
Sumptuous feast had by all so affably

And on a stinking, hot summer's day
Down by the waterhole, kids at play
Loui now had fun teaching everyone
Still the local pun, but never outdone

The Meeting

Coppices of timber and oak cut back
Makes the rainforest wisely decree
Those who gather here unlawfully
If they're caught, will pay a hefty fee

Charlie the eastern dwarf tree frog
Came to a crawl, bypassed the bog
Hopped along and avoided the clog
His presence, he planned, is logged

Charlie saw Cynthia the flying fox
Hoping to stand on a big black box
Swinging through the trees on land
Who'd command the powerful plan?

Here's Peacock the orange butterfly
Dacey the potoroo, so terribly awry
Fluff the pygmy marmoset monkey
Didn't want to appear a real flunky

Snippy the koala perched in his tree
Kahlia the kangaroo stood patiently
Tam, the Tasmanian devil so special
Eager for a swim, but today nestled

All meandered to the meeting place
Tutting and growling without grace
Speaker still unknown, and unseen
They all wanted to vent their spleen

'Hello everyone,' started from Stuey
He'd watched the assembled slowly
'I've thought about this unusual day
And I'm not leading anyone astray.'

So Rabbit raised his whiskered face
'This is our birthplace, we've a case!'
Charlie is agreeing with the speaker
He joined with him about the reaper

'Shall we let him in the forest throng
Try to make him feel he does belong
Ask him to observe our food at bay
Not terrify or cajole, betray or prey?

'He can hunt all day long, be in song
Dance side-by-side at the billabong
Befriend the beautiful red wattlebird
But not to become the forest scourge!

'Bewitch, captivate, enchant, charm
Achieve these things without alarm
Entangle, trick, torment and badger
Cause pain, Fox, you'll be for capture

'Love and treat his brothers as equal
What would be the intriguing sequel?
How awesome it would be and regal
Would he see and blindly let it be.

'Rebellious, unsupervised, untrained
Do we really want our fox to change?
Is his thirst for adventure accessible?
We just want him to become sensible.

'Fox is savvy and wry, no wallflower
To curb his shady behaviour so dour
To even portion a measure of power
With no more prowling on the hour?'

Stuey the rabbit smoothed his throat:
'Fox has scared a big mountain goat
He's quick as a black-tongued snake
Sly and sneaky, always on the make.

The Meeting

'We'll have a vote!' hollered Rabbit
'Ask Fox to rearrange his old habits
Accept the family, watch our forest
To change his ways and be honest!'

Young Fox walked into the meeting
Rabbit offered him a hearty greeting:
'Hi there friend, how are you going?
I had hoped you would be showing.'

'Is this about me and my evil deeds?'
He smiled, he felt genuinely pleased
Wily and spirited, he stood facing all
'Hello everyone,' he slowly drawled

'I hear you're all so very tired of me
Of my escapades, of taking no pleas
I'm a fox, forever it will be like that
You want me to change my combat?

'You all demand I stop, but it's hard
What'll happen if I'm not in charge?
Lorded over and no more will I use
Skills our ancestors used, our roots

'I'm the best, shrewd and quite cute
I hunt by night, my hearing is astute
This is what foxes do, I do it so well
My cubs are growing, will raise hell.'

So angry with him, Kahlia eyed Fox
As he stood proudly on the soapbox
'You should stop and leave us alone
Beware Fox, it's also our forest home.'

The angry plea didn't go unnoticed
Fox went quiet, looked and focused
'If I give my word you'll all be safe
Will it be enough to stop the chafe?'

Kahlia, a doe-eyed pretty kangaroo
Desperately wanted a breakthrough
'There is enough food for everyone
We'll share our spoils, sit in the sun.'

Silence and everyone looked at Fox
Who was deep in thought, on the box
Tam and Snippy, first paws so raised
Say to give it a try, and were praised

Fox now has acquired many friends
Even the humble skittish marsh hens
Rumours are Fox has really changed
He now frequents the faraway grange

Land so fresh and green in the hills
Soft and lush, flushed with the spills
To help Fox change, it was decreed
To give him land so he will succeed

High up on the hill sits Fox and cubs
Enjoying the meal of beef and grubs
Happy and protected, so unexpected
The forest is once again so respected

Tweaks

Striding down the busy, dirty laneway
With unruly blonde hair and in a daze
This sturdy little boy was curiously coy
He swivelled the cobblestones annoyed

Clothes all askew, habitually crinkled
Topsy-turvy, was never one to mingle
On his way home he began to shudder
As a ship in the night without a rudder

Tweaks is his name, and fine indeed
As important as the family title deed
Seven years old and learning to swim
He stopped, body shook in every limb

Next door neighbour's dog, Marmadoo
Surly scoundrel, darted right through
As he pounced up to nervous Tweaks
It produced a bleeding wound or two

Caused such bewilderment he knew
In total turmoil he bit clean through
Up to the hospital he was driven to
The doctors repaired the jerky tissue

Treasure chest of strange syndromes
Little Tweaks eventually went home
Walks to school, listened for the bell
Decided wholeheartedly not to dwell

Awards galore in embellished dreams
Important offers to join the best team
Best and fairest in ticker tape parades
His future paid for, and good grades

'It's only a name,' Tweaks muttered
'Cast it out,' said his brain in a flutter
A more determined and unselfish lad
Tweaks thought he'd end up a nomad

His marks were glaringly abominable
Concentration consistently deplorable
Standing lonely at the school canteen
Socially inept as a stray, stringy bean

Tweaks quietly confided to a stranger
His longing to work as a forest ranger
To fight forest fires, preserve wildlife
Be at peace with nature in the twilight

Stranger he was, but not for very long
Convincing Tweaks that he belonged
Studied long into the night, he toiled
Plied his strengths, failure was foiled

He pursued Tweaks to openly commit
Calmly, Tweaks had to quietly admit
Without his well planned intervention
There would've been total suspension

So true to his name of simply Tweaks
Legs started to disappointingly sneak
From one side to the quivering other
These times he felt like an utter freak

Ignoring these peaks so long overdue
Told his legs they simply have the flu
As still useable, very quick to the step
But now decided to strut the two-step

'I'm not having a bar of this, I insist,'
Tweaks declared in a passionate hiss
'Stop now or I'll promptly shutdown
You're setting me up to be a clown!'

Relentless legs slowly touched down
Overhead arms tumbled and frowned
Moving as if they were born and bred
Outsmarting the other, causing dread

'It's only a name,' he screamed aloud
Wishing it would make him so proud
Escaping from the curious bystanders
And Tweaks begins to eerily meander

Arms and head, try to move smoothly
'No need for brakes,' said so moodily
Was it meant to be, it was all so awry
A sizeable tussle with the inner thigh

Head wanted to go every which way
Shoulders favoured to go just halfway
Legs truthfully showed a lack of tact
Now moving fast as a fuming maniac

Coming to a head in a hugely bad fall
Fanfare of movement instantly at call
Definitely needed an urgent overhaul
Time it now stopped, once and for all

Tweaks lay on the hard, cold ground
Blind to the quiet, swarming surround
When awake he was faint and distant
Simply unable to give any resistance

Stumbling and faint, he tried to stand
Pain had gone, it felt like a backhand
Helplessly, he noticed with suspicion
'I'm not in any acceptable condition.'

Deathly quiet with inner self-loathing
Tweaks looked around, mind groping
Nothing to claim, and so full of shame
He considered, who could be blamed?

Tweaks went to college, met a nice girl
His life on display, like a delicate pearl
Mastered the elite sport of water polo
Given his trophy, his name on the logo

Good at sports, in demand, respected
Dreams from the past he had rejected
No more left out, he quietly reflected
Unforeseen turn of life, now corrected

Tweaks looked up at the clear blue sky
Curious and wondrous to 'just why'
Ranger he was, to his earnest delight
He worked all day and into the night

Girlfriend from college, a lifetime ago
Loved Tweaks's native, wild forests so
He's so gentle with the forest animals
She loved him so, he made her tremble

Arriving in a hurry to view the world
Thrashing and screaming, sheets swirl
Flynn arrived just after the slow dawn
Adored and loved, Flynn just yawned

With a knowing smile, little baby Flynn
Accepted his name as a true champion
His life was full of happiness and love
Not one to complain if life was tough

Having a name with no conventionality
Is flawed and an absolute abnormality
Tweaks had wanted to quietly disclaim
His life now happy, he couldn't blame

www.ingramcontent.com/pod-product-compliance
Lightning Source LLC
Chambersburg PA
CBHW021107080526
44587CB00010B/423